THE MARINERS
OF
NEWPORT
Pembrokeshire

THE MARINERS

OF

NEWPORT

Pembrokeshire

Dillwyn Miles

Gwasg Dinefwr Press

A CIP catalogue record for this book is
available from the British Library.

ISBN 1-904323-12-X

Printed and published in Wales by
Gwasg Dinefwr Press Ltd.
Rawlings Road, Llandybie
Carmarthenshire
SA18 3YD

Cover illustration:
Parrog, the port of Newport.

Contents

Preface

This book has grown out of a list of names of the mariners of Newport sent to me by Dr Reginald Davies, who is engaged in the preparation of a maritime history of north Pembrokeshire. He had collected the names from records held at the National Archives at Kew for his *Index of Welsh Mariners*, now available on website: www.welshmariners.org.uk. He encouraged me to make use of any information contained in the list, or any that he would 'pass on to me about these seafarers.' I am most grateful to Dr Davies for all his help.

Assistance in the preparation of the book has been generously provided by Professor Harold Mytum of the University of York, who provided me with copies of the inscriptions on the gravestones of mariners in the graveyards at St Mary's Church and Ebenezer and Brynberian Chapels, by the Pembrokeshire County Library, the Pembrokeshire Record Office, the National Library of Wales, and by individuals including Edwina Adams, Jeremy Barr, Dr John Beer, Ralph Beer, Dr Deri Bowen, Joanna Bowen, Aelwen Carling, Arthur Davies, David Berrington Davies, Margaret Davies, Patricia Davies, Robin Evans, Llewellyn George, Peter George, Anne Goss, Betty Griffiths, Jean Griffiths, Essex Havard, John Havard CBE, Leonard Harries, Joan Hughes, Sheila James, Jill Jenkins, Martin R. Jones, the late Eira Lacey, Bettye Kirkwood, Geoffrey Lewis, the late Lois Lewis, Tony and Eiry Lewis, Emily Mason, Robert Mason, Herbert Miles, the late Vera Morgan, John Morris, John P. Morris, John Rees, the late Vernon Rees, Derek Richards, Julian Richardson, Luke Rowlands, the late Grace Scurlock, the late Robert Southall, Roland Thorne, Stephen van Dulken, Derek Varney, Lawrence Varney, Mary Varney, Ivor Williams and Kay Williams, to all of whom I wish to express my gratitude, and especially to Enid Davies whose retentive nonagenarian memories of Newport are the only ones I could find that go back beyond mine.

Any student of the maritime history of west Wales is beholden to Dr J. Geraint Jenkins whose *Maritime Heritage* and his many other contributions are the standard works on the subject.

In particular my debt is due to my son, Anthony, who has assisted me in a number of ways, and to Judith, who has endured the time I spent with the mariners without complaint.

While every effort has been made to obtain the correct information, any errors that may appear in the book should be attributed to the author.

Dillwyn Miles

Names in **bold** in the text refer to mariners listed in 'They that went down to the sea', pp. 28-104.

The Port of Newport

There was a time, not a hundred years ago, when the settlements along the north Pembrokeshire coast were largely the haunts and habitations of men of the sea, many of them retired brimful of garnered memories. Those who had sailed the deep seas spoke with familiarity of the streets of New Orleans and Valparaiso, of Singapore and Shanghai, and brought home curios and peculiarities from distant lands. Others, who had followed the coastal trade, remembered tempestuous seas off the storm-beaten headlands of Strumble and St Ann's, or the treachery of the dark troubled waters of Jack Sound and Ramsey.

One such habitation, lying on the drowned estuary of the river Nevern and sheltered from the prevailing winds by Pen Dinas and from northern gales by Morfa Head, provided a landfall for seafarers from prehistoric time.[1] It was descriptively called Trefdraeth, 'a settlement by a sandy shore'. The stretch of land at the navigable limit of the river was named Parrog.[2]

Early in the twelfth century the Welsh hundred of Cemais, extending along the coast from the Gwaun to the Teifi and back to the ridges of the Presely Hills, was occupied by the Norman invader Robert FitzMartin, whose family already held lands in the south-west of England. His successors built a castle overlooking the estuary and planted a new town below it which they called *Novus burgus*, or Newburgh and, later, Newport, still meaning 'a new town', that became the *caput* of the lordship of Cemais. In order to maintain contact with their kith and kin in the south-west, they undoubtedly made use of the port of Newport for sea communication and for commercial and other activities. By the thirteenth century there were demands to provide for the needs of the king, Edward I, in his campaign in north Wales. On 16 March 1283, 'the burgesses and merchants of Cemais having victuals of any sort for sale,' were commanded 'to cause them to be taken near the coast of Merioneth, there to be exposed to sale for the use of the king and of his sub-

jects.' On 31 January 1297 they were instructed 'not to permit anyone to pass the sea from that port without the king's special licence'
and in April that year they received a 'request and order to have all
ships of that port of the burthen of forty tuns of wine and upwards
before the king at Winchelsea on the morrow of midsummer next to
set out to such place as the king should then order' and in July there
was a demand for ships which had returned from Gascony to be
available for passage to Flanders. On 10 May 1342 they were again
cautioned 'to make diligent scrutiny of all those who come to that
port for a passage of whom suspicion may be entertained.'[3]

Maritime activity during the Tudor period was mostly confined to
coastal trading, apart from visits to Bristol and Ireland. Trade was
hampered by the piracy that took place along the Welsh coast almost
without hindrance. There was no power, or perhaps inclination, to
subject shipping to supervision and, in most of the coastal com-
munities, there were those who were ready to supply pirate vessels
with stores, and to buy goods they offered for sale.[4] The Tudors
endeavoured to establish law and order and to improve the defences
of the coast and regulate Welsh maritime affairs by appointing
a Vice-Admiral in each coastal county. The administration of the
customs revenue was reorganized in 1559 and the coastline was
parcelled into legal ports. Newport came under the head port of Milford and the deputy head port of Cardigan. Under Queen Elizabeth
a royal commission was appointed 'for the surveying and ordering
of all creeks, havens and landing places' in Wales, county by county.
The commissioners nominated to survey the coast of the county of
Pembroke were Arnold Butler of Coedcenlas, John Bradshaw of St
Dogmael's, Thomas Catharne of Prendergast, and John Rastall,
Justice of the Great Sessions. Butler died before the survey could
begin, and Bradshaw moved to Radnorshire, leaving Catharne and
Rastall to undertake the survey, which they completed on 8 January
1566. They drew particular attention to the presence within Milford
Haven of a pirate ship of about 60 tons with 40 men on board which
had recently taken two barques and was likely to do more harm as
there was no shipping artillery or ammunition available with which
to apprehend the pirates. A similar complaint was made to the Privy
Council in 1630 regarding a pirate vessel that blocked the mouth of
Milford Haven, but the piracy continued.[5]

There is evidence to show that coal and limestone were brought into the area from the south of the county early in the fifteenth century but there is no record of ships trading along the north Pembrokeshire coast until the latter half of the sixteenth century when some eighteen vessels are known to have belonged to Pembrokeshire ports. The only vessel cited along the north Pembrokeshire coast was *Le Savoir de Newberg in Kames* 6 tons that 'useth commonly to trade to Ireland, North Wales and uppe Severne afishinge.' It was owned by Owen Picton of Trellyffaint, a burgess and merchant of Newport, with Henry Roberts, master, and a crew of three. Between Easter 1566 and Michaelmas 1567, *Le Savior* is known to have traded with Bristol:

18 July 1566, sailed for Bristol with a pack and a fardel [bundle] of friezes [coarse woollen cloth with a nap on one side only] and 11,000 slate stones.

16 August 1566, arrived from Bristol with a ton and a hogshead of iron, 2 hogsheads of train [whale oil], 1 barrel of tar, 2½ tons of pitch, ½ hundredweight hops, ½ hundredweight alum [for dying cloth], 1 quarter. white soap, 1 bolt of poldavi [a coarse canvas woven at Poldavid, near Douarnenez, in Brittany, for use as sailcloth], 1 chest of dry wares, 1 barrel of teasels, 14 bows, 1 fardel of linen, 3 barrels salt and a hundredweight of hops.

12 September 1567 arrived from Bristol with a ton and a hogshead of iron, 3 tons salt, 1 bolt of poldavi, 4 hundredweight pitch, 1 ballet [small ball] of *crassum* [coarse thread, presumably for sewing sailcloth], 1 quarter of hops, ½ hundredweight black soap, 2 dozen hand cards.[6]

The nature of the imported goods indicates that they were required for the construction and maintenance of ships and for the woollen industry carried on in the town. Salt was used for curing meat and herrings, and hops to brew beer. The exports were the products of the woollen factories, and slate quarried from the sea cliffs between Pen Catman and Aber Rhigian, which was of such quality that it was exported to Haverfordwest, Pembroke and Tenby and various parts of Ireland. Slate from these cliff quarries were also used to build the quay walls on the Parrog.

Economic growth during the latter part of the sixteenth century encouraged the expansion of the coastal trade. By 1600 the number of vessels trading in Pembrokeshire had increased to twenty-six, most of them of 20 tons or less in burthen, which led the Elizabethan historian, George Owen of Henllys, lord of Cemais, to complain that 'the county, especially of late years, is fallen much to trade to sea and a great part of the county's people are seamen and mariners, which may not be taken up for land services.'[7] Cloth provided two-thirds of the exports in 1566 but the industry then began to decline and the export of raw wool took its place. Owen found it 'lamentable to see and remember how the trade of clothing used in times past is now utterly neglected,' despite the fact that, by his estimation, 'there is twice as much wool shorn in Pembrokeshire as was forty years past, and then all occupied and wrought within the shire and sold in friezes, but now all sold unwrought.'[8]

'The fishing of Pembrokeshire,' Owen wrote, 'is one of the chiefest worldly commodities wherewithal God has blessed this county, which are of divers sorts taken at divers times of the year and at divers places.'[9] Four centuries earlier Giraldus Cambrensis had written of the quantity and quality of the salmon in the Welsh rivers, declaring that 'the noble river Teifi abounds more than any other river of Wales with the finest salmon,[10] and Owen confirmed that 'the river of Nevern at Newport' was well stocked with salmon that were taken 'in a draught net sometimes by the score at a draught and also in salmon weirs whereof there are three or four on the river.' The burgesses of Newport held common of piscary, that is, the right to take fish in the river Nevern from its mouth to its confluence with the river Clydach. Fishing for salmon and sewin, or sea trout, was allowed also on Traeth Mawr where fishermen use a seine net.[11]

Herring, however, was the most important fish economically. A rental roll of 1594 stated that herring fishing 'yielded greate commoditie to the inhabitants of the towne' and, about the same time, George Owen boasted of 'the great abundance of herrings taken all along the coast as if the same were enclosed in a hedge of herrings, which being in great store and sold to parts beyond the sea, procure also some store of money.'[12] In 1748 Lewis Morris reported that Fishguard and Newport, between them, 'cured yearly about a thousand barrels of herrings' for export. The Act for the Encouragement of the British White Herring Fishery of 1750 provided a grant of thirty shillings per ton for decked vessels between thirty and eighty tons, and a further Act of 1787 extended it to every barrel of herrings taken by open or half-decked vessels of less than twenty tons, all of which resulted in a rapid growth of the herring industry. Herring fishing continued at Newport until the third decade of the twentieth century.

In the mid-sixteenth century Newport, with twenty households, was much of a size with Fishguard, which had twenty-nine, but the latter had 'a good harbour for barks and ships of small burthen', while Newport suffered from 'a barred haven to serve a small ship with a westerly or northerly wind upon a string.'[13] Lewis Morris, in his *Plans of Harbours, Bars, Bays and Roads in St George's Channel*, which he had surveyed in 1748, reported that 'this bar is now very dangerous by the River's being drove to the Rocks on the South Side; there are old piles to be seen at low water mark where the Bar hath formerly been, and where it still ought to be' and he suggested that the 'rolling of Porcupines over the Sand to bring the River into its original Channel is the only Improvement that can be made here at present'.[14]

From the eighteenth century onward the main imports were coal, culm and limestone. Domestic coal was brought from Swansea or Llanelli, as the anthracite of south Pembrokeshire was not suitable for open fires. Culm, which is anthracite coal dust, was imported mostly from Hook. It was mixed with water and dried clay so that it looked like black mortar and this was moulded by hand into egg-shaped 'balls' that were laid on the fire. Before retiring at night, a spadeful of culm was placed on top of the fire and a hole made with a poker in its middle, out of which emerged a blue flame, and the fire kept burning all night. The acid soil of north Pembrokeshire required lime and limestone, brought mostly from the West Williamston quarries, was burned in lime kilns that were built in almost every creek and harbour, and Newport had the largest concentration on the north coast. The limestone, George Owen wrote:

> . . . being dug in the quarry in great stones is hewn lesser to the bigness of a man's fist, and less, to the end they might the sooner

burn through, and being hewn small the same is put in to a kiln made of wall six foot high, four or five foot broad at the brim but growing narrower to the bottom, having two loop holes in the bottom which they call the kiln eyes. In this kiln first is made a fire of coal, or rather culm, which is but the dust of the coal, which is laid in the bottom of the kiln, and some few sticks of wood to kindle the fire. Then is the kiln filled with these small pieces of limestone, and then fire being given, the same burns for the space of [blank] and makes the limestone to become mere red fiery coals, which being done and the fire quenched, the lime so burnt is suffered to cool in the kiln, and then is drawn forth through these kiln eyes, and in this sort is carried to the land where it is laid in heaps and the next shower of rain makes it moulder and fall into dust which they spread on the land, and so sow wheat or barley therein as the time of the year require.[15]

The kiln was normally built against a bank that served as a platform from which horse-drawn carts could unload the limestone into the kiln. Limestone burning continued at Newport until about 1920 when lime was replaced by imported fertilisers, such as guano and superphosphates. Slaked lime was also used to lime wash the walls and grouted roofs of farmhouses, cottages and outbuildings.

The proceedings of the Newport Court Leet, from the middle of the eighteenth century onward, reveal that consent for the erection of lime kilns on common land on, or near, the Parrog was granted to various merchants and landowners for the purpose of developing maritime trade. James Bowen of Llwyngwair and Thomas Knolles of Wenallt were given permission to erect a lime kiln at Penybont in 1751. Thomas Mathias was allowed to build one on the Parrog in 1777 and William Warren of Trewern had consent to erect one at the end of Lower St. Mary Street. Permission was also given for a lime kiln to be built in the High Street, now Market Street, but there is no evidence that this was done. Early maps shows three lime kilns on the Parrog (two of which were wantonly destroyed), two at the bottom of Lower St Mary Street, two at the end of Long Street, one on The Marsh and one on the other side of the river near Bryncyn.

Grants of land were also made for the erection of storehouses on the Parrog. John Lloyd obtained consent to enclose land on which to build a storehouse of four couples in 1758 and his son, John

Lloyd, had permission thirty years later to 'build a small storehouse for the use of lime burners to sleep.' John James had 'liberty to build a storehouse on the Parrog' in 1759, and **Essex Bowen** had consent to enclose a yard along side his storehouse in the following year. **William Lloyd** was allowed to extend his storehouse on the Parrog by fourteen feet in 1792. On 13 May 1796, the Court gave permission to David Harries of Newport to build 'a storehouse 40 foot long and 25 foot in breadth in the south-west of William Lloyd's storehouse that is near the sea shore,' which may be the storehouse that has survived and has been converted as the Newport Boat Club. Consent to build a quay wall was granted in 1816 and, in June 1824, **John Davies** (1766-1835), master mariner and merchant, was allowed to build a quay at Parrog 'between his present warehouse and the sea' and also to build a smithy nearby. In April 1825 **Daniel Evans** (1767-1829), master mariner, and John Jenkins were allowed to connect 'Capt. Evans's New Quay' to that of John Jenkins.

A considerable number of ships are known to have been trading with the port of Newport before 1875 (p. 121) and, between April 1876 and March 1900, a detailed account of vessels arriving has survived in a Boarding Book (p. 123).[16] During that period 104 vessels made 1,466 visits, most of them appearing a number of times. The *Ann & Betsey* 22 tons belonging to **Elizabeth Berriman** was boarded on 229 occasions, and others, like **Jacob Beer**'s *New Providence* and the *Gloucester Packet* belonging to Richard Jackson of the Queen's Hotel, Parrog, were frequent visitors. During the year 1884 no less than 99 ships were boarded, and 85 arrived in 1878 and the same number in 1885. When the tide was high, the ships tied up alongside the quay wall behind Camelot, but otherwise they had to unload on the beach. Apart from the culm, limestone and coal, they also brought building stone, bricks and timber, together with quantities of salt and, more latterly, guano, and artificial fertilisers.

The maritime trade at Newport received a sharp impulsion with the arrival in the town in 1789 of **John Davies**, master mariner, merchant and ship owner. He was a member of a Newport family that had removed to Cardigan and of which it was said that it 'will go down in Welsh history as the entrepreneurs of West Wales commerce in the late eighteenth and early nineteenth centuries.'[17] He married Ann Evans of Newport, where he settled and employed a number of local people in his enterprises. At his death he owned, or had shares in, a number of vessels including the sloops *Aerona*, *Mary* and *Princess Royal*, the brigs *Minerva*, *Ocean*, *Valiant* and *Mary & Eleanor*, and the schooners *Brothers* and *Thetis*. He owned property in Newport including land on the east side of St Mary's Church, and a house in Goat Street, two storehouses, a smithy and a coal yard on the Parrog, together with houses and buildings in St Dogmael's and Cardigan.[17]

The prosperity of the port may be indicated by the number of inns and taverns that flourished on the Parrog and included the *Queen's*, or *Queen's Head, Hotel*, now Morfan, the *Sloop Inn* (Beach View), the *Parrog Arms* (Morawelon), the *Crown and Anchor* (adjoining the destroyed lime kiln facing Camelot), the *Ship Afloat* (Seagull Cottage), and the *Mariners' Arms*, beyond Bettws.

The number of shipwrecks that occurred in the vicinity led to the provision of a Rocket Life-Saving Apparatus that was carried on a two-wheeled hand-cart and, later, on a horse-drawn waggon, to accommodate which a building was erected on the Parrog, near the lime-burner's house, with a mortuary alongside. In 1884 a lifeboat, the gift of a summer visitor from Somerset was launched, and a lifeboat-house was built on land leased from the Llwyngwair estate at Cwm Dewi, but owing to the difficulty of launching the lifeboat, which could only be done at high tide, it ceased to function in 1895. During that time it had only been effectively called out on three occasions but it had saved eleven lives.

Although the maritime trade declined rapidly following the coming of the railway to west Wales in the 1850s, it continued at Newport as there was no convenient railhead until the Whitland and Cardigan railway got to Crymych in 1875, and the Great Western Railway eventually reached Goodwick in 1899.

The little ships continued to bring their cargoes for another thirty years, among the last being the *Thomond* 130 tons owned by Capt. George of Trefin, the *Harparees* 161 tons, wooden screw barge, built at Sittingbourne in 1920, wrecked in 1929, the *Garlandstone* 120 tons built at Calstock on the Tamar for Capt. John Russan of Dale and now owned by the National Museum of Wales. The schooner *Mary Jane Lewis* 25 tons built at Milford in 1899, spent the winter at Newport in 1901 with Thomas Phillips from Pembroke master and a mate and a cook. It also moored there for the winter in 1925, behind Camelot, when small boys were invited on board to listen to Jack the Bosun's tales of the sea and to be taught how to hand-roll, and smoke, cigarettes. The last coal importers were David Luke, for whom the vessel *Anne* 30 tons brought coal which he stored in his coal yard on the Parrog, and J. O. Vaughan, whose schooner *Wave* 130 tons, with **Walter Varney** as master, made regular visits until it was lost at sea. The last shipment, of coal, was delivered by the *Agnes* of Bideford on 19 September 1933.

Shipbuilding at Newport

Newport was a leading shipbuilding port on the north Pembroke-shire coast in the eighteenth and nineteenth centuries. More than twenty shipyards were active in the county at that time, six of which were situated on the north coast. The Shipping Registers for the ports of Milford, Pembroke and Cardigan[18] record that between 1760 and 1850 nineteen ships were built at Fishguard, twelve at St Dogmael's, three at Abercastle, and one each at Goodwick and Cwmyreglwys, while fifty vessels were shown to have been built at Newport, reaching a peak during the 1810-19 decade:

	Ships built	Tonnage
1760-69	1	23 tons
1770-79	3	79 tons
1780-89	1	60 tons
1790-99	4	219 tons
1800-09	8	614 tons
1810-19	15	1,793 tons
1820-29	7	655 tons
1830-39	10	667 tons
1840-49	1	94 tons.

The nature and size of shipyards varied and, not infrequently, a ship would be built on a beach or on land near enough to the sea for it to be launched. The vessel would be built of native oak obtained from nearby woods as long as a supply was available, and after-wards of timber imported from the Baltic or from Nova Scotia and Newfoundland. The construction would be undertaken by local crafts-men: the shipwright would lay the keel and build the vessel carvel-style with the assistance of other craftsmen including blacksmiths who would produce the iron fittings, shackles and anchors, block makers who made pulley blocks of ash and elm of various sizes, sailmakers and ropemakers.

There are no official records of vessels prior to the Shipping Registration Act of 1786. The sloop *Ann & Mary* 22 tons was first registered cat Cardigan in February 1787 but it is known that she was built at Newport in 1762. For more than a hundred years she plied her trade between Milford Haven and the north Pembrokeshire ports, usually carrying limestone and culm, before being lost without trace off St David's Head on 25 April 1873. The *Rose* 25 tons built in 1773, was undoubtedly the vessel to which John Wesley referred in his *Journal* on 28 September 1777 when he wrote that he had 'made straight for Mr Bowen's at Llwyngwair in Pembrokeshire, hoping to borrow his sloop and so cross over to Dublin without delay.'

The inscription on the gravestone of **David Gilbert** (1745-1821) in St Mary's churchyard describes him as 'master of the brig *Ceturah*, and states that the *Ceturah* was 'the first brig built at this port.' It is likely that the vessel was named after his wife, Ceturah (née Lloyd) whom he married in 1774.

The type of vessel most commonly built at Newport in the latter part of the eighteenth century was the sloop, or smack, a single-masted vessel fore-and-aft rigged with topsail and jib that was capable of being unloaded on an open beach. It was then found necessary to build vessels with a deeper keel to sail the deep sea such as the brig, two-masted and square rigged, and the. brigantine with the foremast square rigged and the mainmast fore-and-aft rigged, and also the snow, a square rigged vessel similar to the brig but with a small trysail mast set on a boom abaft. From the 1820s onward, the most popular type of vessel was the schooner, a two-masted vessel fore-and-aft-rigged: and sometimes with square sails placed on the fore-topmast when the vessel was known as a topsail schooner.[19]

The leading shipbuilders at Newport were members of the Havard family (p. 56). **David Havard** (1731-1817), was the son of Owen Havard, farmer and carpenter of Pendre Farm and mayor of Newport in 1757-58. He followed his father, who died in 1758, at Pendre as farmer, and presumably as carpenter, for he was the first person known to have built a ship at Newport. This may have been the *Ann & Mary* built in 1762 and he built the *Rose* in 1773. In 1814 he moved to Dandre. He was followed by his son, **John Havard**

(1771-1839), and his grandson, **Levi Havard** (1812-61), both of whom are described on their gravestones as 'shipbuilder'. They built their ships on, or near, Parrog Bach where they erected a storehouse, and dug a sawpit, on common land for which the family paid chief rent to the barony of Cemais until recent years. The vessels known to have been built by the family between 1773 and 1847 included:

Date	Vessel	Owner	Master
1773	*Rose* sloop 27 tons	Geo Bowen, Llwyngwair	
1777	*Betty* sloop 24 tons	John Jenkins	Llewellyn Jenkins
1790	*William & Anne* sloop 88 tons	John Morris	John Owen
1792	*Elizabeth & Mary* sloop 60 tons	David James	David James
1795	*Flora* sloop 28 tons	David Harries	David Harries
1801	*Fanny Anne* sloop 22 tons	Thos Williams	Thos Williams
1802	*Jupiter* sloop 64 tons	William Evans	William Evans
1804	*Charlotte* schooner 74 tons	David Williams	David Williams
1804	*Culloden* brig 83 tons	John Thomas	John Thomas
1805	*Hope* sloop 21 tons	John Davies	John Isaac
1810	*Mary Anne* sloop 28 tons	Thos Evans	Thos Evans
1810	*Minerva* brig 102 tons	David Havard	David Havard
1811	*Victory* brig 118 tons	Anne Nicholas	Evan Nicholas
1812	*Hope* brig 112 tons		
1812	*Valiant* brig 144 tons	William Owen	William Owen
1814	*Diligence* brig 114 tons	Llewelyn Griffiths	Llewelyn Griffiths
1814	*Eliza* brig 145 tons	Owen Harries	Frederick Seaborne
1816	*Providence* brigantine 163 tons	David James	
1826	*Hope* snow 112 tons		
1826	*Elizabeth* schooner 108 tons	David Williams	
1828	*Brothers* schooner 99 tons	David Evans	
1828	*Grace* schooner 103 tons	William Jenkins	
1829	*Harmony* schooner 95 tons	William Havard	
1831	*Reform* sloop 14 tons		John Havard
1832	*Ocean* brig 120 tons	David Nicholas	David Nicholas
1834	*Agenoria* brigantine 117 tons		William Evans
1835	*Alert* sloop 33 tons		David Griffiths
1835	*Claudia* schooner 103 tons	John Havard	
1837	*Jane* schooner 78 tons		John Morris
1839	*Elizabeth* sloop 27 tons		Llewelyn Jenkins
1839	*Phebe* schooner 123 tons		David Havard
1842	*Anne* brig 161 tons		Wm Havard
1847	*Adroit* schooner 72 tons	George James	George James

William Lloyd, who lived at Bettws before he moved to Penfeidr on the death of his brother, George Lloyd in 1818, contributed to the swollen figure of ships built at Newport during the second decade of the nineteenth century. He built the brig *Artuose* 150 tons in 1814, and the brigantines *Venerable* 128 tons in 1815 and *Ardent* in 1817. He would appear to have been the William Lloyd whom the Court Leet permitted in 1792 to extend his storehouse on the Parrog by fourteen feet, which may have been the storehouse that John Lloyd built in 1758. In his will, proved on 12 November 1833, he left shares in the *Artuose* and other vessels to members of his family at Abercastle. A strong connection between that family and Newport is provided by the will of his niece, Martha Morgan of Abercastle, who died in 1834 leaving shares in the *Ann & Mary*, the *Artruose*, the *Charlotte*, the *Elizabeth & Mary*, the *Valiant* and the *Venerable*, all of which were built at Newport.[20]

The following vessels were also built at Newport but the name of the shipwright in each case remains unknown:

Date	Vessel	Owner	Master
1762	*Ann & Mary* sloop 22 tons		
1774	*Ceturah* brig		David Gilbert
1777	*Providence* sloop 28 tons		
1777	*Fair Briton* sloop 59 tons		
1795	*Eleanor* sloop 41 tons		
1800	*Sampson* brigantine 150 tons	Owen Harries	James Seaborne
1802	*Lord Nelson* snow 113 tons		Llewelyn Griffiths
1804	*Princess Royal* sloop 77 tons		
1814	*Artuose* brig 150 tons	William Lloyd	
1815	*Venerable* brigantine 128 tons	William Lloyd	
1817	*Friendship* brig 83 tons		
1817	*Ardent* brigantine 140 tons	William Lloyd	David Jenkins
1819	*Mary* sloop 53 tons		
1823	*Hope* snow 182 tons		Thos Nicholas, Pendre
1824	*Charlotte* schooner 81 tons		
1825	*Swift* sloop 39 tons		John Mathias
1830	*David*, schooner 26 tons		
1837	*Ann & Betsey* smack 22 tons	Eliz Berriman	
	Fly smack 23 tons on a date unknown.[22]		

By 1847, the prospect of a demand for larger vessels that could not be floated across the bar at the estuary of the river caused **Levi Havard** to remove his shipbuilding business to Castle Pill, Milford. He remained there until he retired in 1858 when he returned to Newport and lived with his widowed sister, Mary Davies, at Dandre. He died on 28 October 1881 and in his obituary it was noted that he 'gave employment to hundreds of his townspeople' and that his 'well known face and kindly advice will be missed by many.'

It was clamed at one time that the last ship to be built at Newport was the schooner *Martha*, the master of which **Owen Evans** (1787-1872) used to take his wife, Nannie, to sea with him as steward, with **David Thomas**, of the Ship Afloat and later of Fern Cottage, as mate. Evans, according to the story, 'used to make a profitable side line by smuggling china crockery which his wife bought in foreign ports.'[21]

Ships were frequently held in joint ownership, usually by a number of people comprising the master and members of his family together with interested parties who had contributed towards the cost of construction of the ship or had supplied the items for its construction and such shares were often given in lieu of payment. Other shareholders would include merchants and, in particular, farmers who would benefit from the use of the vessel in importing culm and coal and limestone and, more latterly, fertilisers. After 1825 it became mandatory for the ownership of a vessel to be held in sixty-four shares and shareholders could hold any number of shares, the number most frequently held being four shares and this was referred to as 'an ounce'. The shares were sometimes bequeathed to relatives or friends. George Bowen of Llwyngwair, in his will dated 29 June 1809, left his sloop *Rose* to his daughters who lived at Berry Hill, and his *Little Hetty*, also a sloop, to his granddaughter, Easter, daughter of the Rev. David Griffiths, vicar of Nevern.

An example of co-ownership is provided in the Certificate of British Registry dated 14 April 1832 relating to the brig *Ocean* of Cardigan 121 tons built by **John Havard** at Newport in that year for **David Nicholas** (1803-77), master mariner, of Mount Pleasant.

Shareholders	*Shares*
David Nicholas (master) of Newport	8
John Davies, merchant of Newport	4 (mother's brother)
John Havard, the shipbuilder	2
David Davies, merchant of Cardigan	12 (mother's brother)
John Griffiths, mariner	4
David Morgan	4
John Thomas, gentleman	4
Mary Bowen, widow, of Tredefaid	4 (cousin)
Elizabeth Bowen, spinster	4
Anne James, widow, Newport	4 (cousin)
Rowland Rowlands, mariner	4 (brother-in-law)
Thomas Nicholas, mariner	2 (father)
Phebe Nicholas, spinster	2 (sister)
Anne Nicholas, spinster	2 (sister)
Margaret Davies, widow	2 (cousin)
William Roberts, shipbuilder, Milford	2 (cousin's husband)

As the completed vessel took to the water, it was customary for a launching ceremony to be held and there are reports of such celebrations taking place in south Ceredigion, when the ship was dressed overall and a bottle broken on the bow. There is no account extant of a ceremony of the kind being held at Newport but the launching of the schooner *Hebog* (Hawk) in the 1770s was celebrated in a poem written to wish the vessel and her owner and crew good fortune as she set out on her first voyage (p. 105).

Locally built vessels were occasionally given unusual names, from those of a descriptive nature such as *Adroit* and *Artuose*, to that of the god *Jupiter*, or the goddess *Agenoria*, whose name, incidentally, was also borne by the GWR engine at Whitland. More often they were named after a wife or a daughter or a sweetheart, and sometimes an attempt was made to please two ladies at the same time, like *Ann & Betsey*, and one wonders whether such fulsome names as the *Charming Nancy* or the *Lovely Peggy* ever won the hand of a maiden. The *Phebe* and the *Anne* built by **John Havard** for his ill-fated sons, **David** and **William**, bore the names of their wives. A vessel built for another son, **John Havard**, who died unmarried, was named *Claudia* and one wonders whether she was his intended bride.

The Mariners of Newport

Beside the shipwrights, the ship builders and the ship owners, there were the men who made the ships ride the seas, the mariners. At one time, they formed a sizeable proportion of the working population of Newport.

Sons followed fathers. The three sons of **David Isaac**, master mariner, became masters of their own ships. **David Lewis** and his four sons were seafarers, and the five sons of **Edward Richards**, marine engineer, were men of the sea. It was not necessary to have a seagoing father, however, for six of the seven sons of Jesse Varney, gardener, became mariners.

That local mariners and master mariners are not infrequently found serving on the same ship bespeaks a camaraderie within the community. A young lad would be taken to sea as an apprentice by, or under the protection of, a master mariner who was a relative, a neighbour or a friend. **Owen Williams** was so taken as an apprentice by **William Isaac**, Gwylfa, to whom he was related. Such an opportunity provided no surety of any special treatment, however, as revealed by **William Thomas Jermain** who sailed on the *Ondara* with **Thomas Williams**, 'a pretended friend of my widowed mother', and was so badly treated and poorly fed that he got off the ship at the first opportunity. **John Owen** (1802-42) not only signed on as an apprentice with **Daniel Evans** (1767-1829) master of the *Valiant* but went on to serve with local master mariners **Thomas Morris** on the *William & Anne*, and **John Williams** on the *Jupiter.*

Families knew each other and it could happen that a master chose a member, or members, of his crew before he left home. **David Wood** of Tyrhedyn, master of the barque *Lucia*, may well have engaged **Josiah Lloyd** and **John Salmon Gilbert** in this manner. On the other hand, men would seek to serve under a known, and especially a respected, master. **David John** could have persuaded **John Morris**, Ivy House, to take him as mate on the *Jane Morrison* in 1856, and **William Williams** (1833-67), who lived a few doors away, may have sought to be his second mate on the *Xiphias* later that year, and **John Davies**, Fountain Cottage, to be mate from 1859 to 1861. There was no prearrangement, however, when two brothers happened to join the same ship and then found that the master was their eldest brother (p. 98).

There are instances of a succession of local men appearing as masters of the same ship. The barque *Ondara*, in which **Thomas Williams** (1812-69) had acquired a major share, was under his command from 1858 to 1862. **Thomas Griffiths** (1830-74), who had been mate on the ship in 1858-60, was master in 1862-65. **Thomas Williams** resumed command during 1865 and 1866 and his son-in-law, **David Mathias**, succeeded him from 1867 to 1870. The vessel left Swansea for Tabasco on 11 June 1870 with **Watkin Thomas** as master, but she had to be abandoned at sea and the master and some of the crew were drowned. The personal connections here are traceable but this is less so in the case of the *Madawaska* of Milford which also had a series of Newport master mariners in command: **David Thomas** (1819-87) from 1859 to 1861, **William Williams** (1813-64) from 1863 to 1864 and then **William Thomas Jermain** took the vessel to the Gulf of Mexico and back to Milford. **Thomas Williams**, rather than staying in command of his own ship, the *Ondara*, became master of the *Madawasks* from 1867 until the ship was wrecked in the following year.

Some sailors sailed in small ships in coastal waters, usually carrying culm and limestone from the south of the county, while others navigated the deep sea and were away from home for long periods at a time. They would sail for a hundred days without sight of land and then face the perilous passage round the Horn. **Thomas George Evans**, however, thought that he would save time by sailing through the Straits of Magellan and, we were always told, his hair turned white in a night.

Mariners had to face the perils of the sea at all times, and nowhere more so than off the coasts of Wales. **Daniel Evans** (1801-77) and the two-man crew of the *Miss Sarah* were drowned when the vessel foundered off St Ann's Head. **Gabriel Jenkins** and his young son went down with the smack *Fly* almost within sight of home. Most, however, met their death in distant places. **John Morgan** was drowned off St Petersburg, **Thomas Meyrick Evans** off Pondicherry. **William Owen** of the *Mary Ellen* died in Quebec in 1846, which marked the beginning of a link with America. There were also connections with South America. **Albert Bowen** died at Monte Video and **John Lloyd Davies** died at Santa Fé and **Thomas Davies**, **David James**, **David Thomas** and **Henry Thomas** died variously at Rio de Janeiro. **William Eynon** died on the west coast of Africa and **John Richards** died in Ceylon. Families were brought down. **John Davies** (1766-1835) had three sons and a son-in-law drowned at sea. **John Havard** (1771-1838) lost three sons and two sons-in-law. **Evan Nicholas** lost his father and his brother and his two sons, aged twelve and fifteen years, at sea. The day in January 1894 when the *Afon Cefni* foundered with her master, **John Hughes**, and crew of seven Newport men, was long remembered.

War, wherever it took place, touched the neighbourhood. In 1812 **William Davies** (1775-1863) had his snow *Eliza* captured by the French and he and his crew were held prisoner in a French port. **Llewelyn Davies**'s brig *Alliance*, on a voyage from Cork to Limerick in August 1813, was set on fire by the American brig-of-war *Argus*. **John Morris** lost his ship in the Crimean War. **Johnny Davies**'s vessel, the *Stanwell*, was bombed and set on fire in the Spanish Civil War. In the war of 1914-18 ships were torpedoed and sunk by submarine and by zeppelin. The commemorative tablet in the Memorial Hall bears the names of thirty-five local men who lost their lives in that war, of whom fifteen were mariners. The tablet commemorating those who fell in the 1939-45 war has twenty-seven names of which fifteen, again, were sailors.

Gravestones erected in memory of mariners are, of necessity, few. They represent those who died on land, although some who were lost at sea or died elsewhere have their names inscribed, usually alongside those of other members of the family. Most of those commemorated in this way are master mariners. It also has to be remembered that raising a tombstone was beyond the means of most mariners' familes. From a historian's point of view, the inscriptions on the gravestones are disappointing, usually giving the description of the deceased as no more than 'mariner of this town'. Only rarely is the address given, or the name of the ship, the space being occupied by Biblical verses or some form of epitaph.

The sea also brought joy in the form of matrimonial alliances.

The families of Bowen, Davies, James, Mathias and Seabornes were related by marriage, and so were those of Williams, Thomas, Griffiths, Shadrach and Morris. Havard and Nicholas and Rowlands also had close marital connections.

In a small community the welfare of those at sea was of prime concern. A casual meeting on the street would invariably elicit an enquiry regarding the welfare and whereabouts of a relative serving on a ship. The local newspapers, *The County Echo* and the *Cardigan and Tivyside Advertiser*, would regularly contain references to the homecoming, or departure for sea, of one or more Newport mariners. Once a mariner had left home there would be little opportunity to make contact with his family until he returned. Sailors were not always regular correspondents and letters took a long time to travel and, as a rule, families were unaware of the location of ships at any one time and had no easy means of finding it until the *Western Mail* began to publish a column headed 'Movements of Vessels' and a copy was placed daily in the Reading Room at the Memorial Hall (p. 47).

Most mariners, when they retired, chose to live quietly, but some remained active in one way or another. Pigot's Commercial Directory for 1830 lists **John Davies**, **Daniel Evans** and **David James**, retired master mariners, as the only three merchants in the town, and in the 1880 Slater's Directory, **John James**, Westleigh, is shown as 'Wine & Spirit Merchant'. **William Evans**, Cross House, opened a coal merchant's business in the latter part of the nineteenth century. Master mariners were shown respect and were addressed at all times as Captain So-and-so. Some took part in civic life and a number of master mariners held the office of mayor of the town and corporation of Newport. Among those who served in that office were **Daniel Evans**, 1825-26, **Thomas Harries**, Pendre, 1843-45, **William Evans**, 1850-52, **William Evans**, Cross House, 1878-80, **William Davies**, Commercial Hotel, 1898-99, **Levi Griffiths**, Mauritius, 1899-1901, **John Meyrick**, Mount Pleasant, 1901-02, **Henry Rees Felix**, 1904-06, **David Mathias**, Ondara, 1906-08, **David Jones**, Ivy House, 1908-10, **John Davies**, Fern Cottage, 1911-12, and **Morris John Morgan**, 1972-74.

They that went down to the sea

The mariners of Newport whose names are remembered are listed below. Much of the material relating to their sailing comes from Board of Trade records held at The National Archives, Kew, and was collected by Dr Reginald Davies for his Index of Welsh Mariners *which, in the main, comprises the names of Welshmen who had obtained certificates of competency by examination from 1850 to 1945. More detailed information can be seen at the* Index *website:* www.welshmariners.org.uk *designed by Nigel Callaghan of Technoleg Taliesin. Dr Davies's list contained 450 names but, with the addition of more names found by him in his further researches, together with those obtained by the author by local enquiry and personal knowledge and recollection, it now contains 630 names.*

Names marked with an asterisk (*) are buried or remembered in St Mary's churchyard, Newport.

George Picton Adams* (1886-1951), Westfield, Parrog, son of John Adams, Rock House, was a marine engineer. He had to take to the lifeboat when his ship, the SS *Ellington*, sank off the coast of Spain in March 1922 and managed to reach the port of Vigo. He was later chief engineer on the Mosquito Line trading with Aruba. After his retirement he was a keen yachtsman and was prominent in the local annual regatta with his sailing boat, *Glenys*, named after his elder daughter, winning all the races. He married Nellie Griffiths, daughter of The Farm, now Eastfield, and died in 1951. His son, **David Adams**, was an engineer on the Irish Cross-Channel vessels and later marine superintendent at Fishguard harbour. He was married to Edwina Evans, Bon Marché. He died in 1992.

Thomas Davies Adams, marine engineer, who had settled at St Dogmael's, was a brother of George Adams.

Llewellyn (Lynn) Adams, Glantraeth, Penybont, was a marine engineer with the Shell Oil Line.

Reudolph Anderson, mariner, of Gate House, West Street, was one of the so-called Russian-Finns who came to fell trees in the

Llwyngwair Woods during the 1914-18 war. Like some of his compatriots, he married and settled locally.

Jacob Beer (1846-1922), a native of Gorran Haven, near Mevagissey, settled at Hakin. In 1873 he was married at Hubberston parish church to Catherine Mathias Thomas who had been born at Newport and baptised at Tabernacle Calvinistic Methodist Chapel. She had previously been married and had a son, David Davies, and before that, was the wife of **Rees Thomas** (1810-66). In about 1893, after a period keeping a shop at Haverfordwest, the couple moved to Newport and lived in two houses in West Street, in one of which they may have had a shop. He was master and owner of a number of ships trading with Newport during the last quarter of the nineteenth century, including the smack *Rechabite* 18 tons, the sloop *Aeron* 17 tons, the 28 ton dandy *Newland*, the sloop *Good Hope* 27 tons, the schooner *Cristal*, and his wife's schooner *New Providence* 31 tons which visited Newport more than ninety times between 1884 and 1899. After his wife's death in 1909, he moved to Sandy Haven where he died in 1922 and was buried in St Ishmael's churchyard. The *Cristal* gave its name to the character 'Captain Cristal' in R. M. Lockley's *Dream Island*, and the stark hulk of the vessel lying at Sandy Haven is featured by Graham Sutherland on the dust jacket of his autobiographical work, *The World of Graham Sutherland*. Jacob's father, George Beer* (1816-94), master and owner of the *Urgent* and of the *Danzig*, spent his latter years with his son and died at Newport in October 1894.

Richard Berriman* (1813-47), Prospect House, Parrog, master mariner, was the owner of the smack *Ann & Betsey* 22 tons and of the sloop *David* 35 tons, both built at Newport. He and his family are commemorated in the Good Shepherd stained glass window in the chancel of St Mary's Church. His daughter, **Mary Elizabeth Berriman**, born in 1844, grew to manage her father's business with efficiency. The *Ann & Betsey* brought 229 cargoes of coal, culm and limestone, far more times than any other ship, to Newport between 1876 and 1899. She also owned the *Exley* 21 tons that was wrecked off Strumble Head in 1871 and the 18 ton smack *Richard & Mary* that ran ashore at Bettws in 1854. She lived at Victoria Lodge, Upper West Street, which has a row of cottages running up behind the house called Berriman Terrace. She was described in a trade directory in 1880 as 'a lime-burner' indicating that she owned, or leased, one of the lime kilns. She is remembered as a stately, but stern, old lady in a coloured shawl and a black straw hat.

John Beynon, born *c.*1782, was an ordinary seaman serving on HMS *Caesar* at the battle of Trafalgar.

Thomas Beynon, Waunorfa, born in 1839, sailed as mate on the *Terra Nova* to the Americas 1875-81 and was master of the *Merle* in which he sailed from London on 3 September 1884 for Cape Town and returned to Liverpool from the East Indies on 2 February 1886. His son, **William Beynon**, died of typhoid on 29 June 1925 whilst serving as steward on the *H. H. Asquith* and was buried at Bahia, Brazil. His grandson, **Jack Beynon**, who was a steward, married Gwladys Davies, Fountain Hill, and lived at Penybont.

Albert Bowen* (1850-1902) was master of the *Chilean* 1876-86 and master and owner of the *Arctic Stream* from 1886. He married Emma, daughter of **John James** (1808-1902), master mariner, Westleigh, by whom he had a son, George Bowen, who was a medical practitioner at Haverfordwest. He died in Monte Video following a tempestuous passage round Cape Horn.

Essex Bowen (1734-1811), Captain, Royal Marines, of Llwyngwair, appears to have been involved in the maritime trade after he retired from the Marines for he was given consent by the Court Leet in 1793 to enclose a plot of land for use as a yard adjoining a storehouse which he already owned on the Parrog. He was mistakenly identified locally as the Captain Essex Bowen featured in an article in the magazine *Britannia and Eve* in October 1937, who took Anne, the orphan daughter of Lord Talbot, with him to war disguised as a drummer boy.

John Bowen (1786-1832), master of the *Heart of Oak* of Cardigan.

John Bowen, born in 1808, was mate on the *Gannet* in 1859.

Thomas Bowen (1787-1822), master of the sloop *Neptune*, was drowned on 5 December 1822.

William Bowen, born in 1791, was an able seaman serving on HMS *Conqueror* at the battle of Trafalgar.

Arthur James Charles, Cross House, served on the *Daphnella*, the *Diplodon* and the *Natacina* of the Royal Dutch Shell group and spent some time in Hong Kong. He married Margaret Lewis (née Thomas), Central Café.

William Edward Cheverton (1885-1912), Mill Lane, a native of the Isle of Wight, was steward on the *Titanic* that foundered on 13 April 1912.

William Cole was mate on the *Ann & Betsey* bringing coal from Landshipping to Newport in 1861.

Richard Myles Cox, born in 1857, was master of the *Anerley* 1884-87 and of the *Twickenham* in 1888.

Eric Daniel, Mount Pleasant, master mariner, was a grandson of **Thomas Griffiths** of Cnwce, master of the *Ocean Gem*, and a cousin of the seafaring sons of **Edward William Richards**, Mount Pleasant Terrace.

John Daniel (1869-92), mate on the *Blaenavon*, was drowned in March 1892 and his body was washed ashore at Malahide, co. Dublin.

Benjamin Davies (1762-1849), master mariner, married Mary, daughter of the **Rev. Stephen Lloyd**, owner of the sloop *Mayflower*, and had a son, John Davies (1810-80), who was ordained in 1843 at Gideon Independent Chapel, Dinas, where he ministered while carrying on his trade as a shoe-maker at Newport for the next 35 years.

Benjamin Davies (1831-87), Castle Street, was master of the *Colombo* that was lost at sea in 1874, and of the *Phoenix* 1883-87. He died at Santos, Brazil, on 14 July 1887. He and his brothers, **Thomas Davies** (1825-76) and **David Davies**, master of the *Amcott*, moved to Durham and Northumberland.

Benjamin Davies, master and owner of the 24 ton smack *Jane & Margaret* in 1876.

Caleb Davies, born in 1843, was master of the *Artizan* 1877-84, the *Auriga* 1884-87 and of the *Vivid* in 1887.

Daniel Davies, born in 1843, was mate on the *Catherine* from 1882 to 1887 and on the *Greyhound* 1887-88.

David Davies* (1815-55), Dandre, master mariner, kept a journal on a voyage he made to Madeira in the *Britannia*. He married Mary, daughter of **John Havard** (1771-1839) and died on 6 October 1855 at Limerick where a wake was held before his body was brought home for burial in St Mary's churchyard.

David Davies, born in 1817, mate on the *Joseph Steel*, was discharged at Calcutta in 1860.

David Davies, born in 1838, was master of the *Amcott* 1878-9 and of the *Regal* 1881-88 sailing to the Mediterranean. In 1881 he and his family lived at Bishopwearmouth. He erected a tombstone in St Mary's churchyard in memory of his mother, Maria Davies, Castle Street, who died on 18 November 1878, aged 85 years. He was a brother of **Thomas Davies** (1825-76) and of **Benjamin Davies** (1831-87).

David Davies (1849-79), mate on the *Delta*, was drowned when the vessel was run down on 18 February 1879.

David Davies, born in 1859, was master of the *Glenavon* 1886-88.

David Davies was master of the 27 ton smack *Margaret Ellen* at Newport in 1882.

David Davies, seaman, lost his life during the 1914-18 war.

David Gilbert Davies* of West Street was drowned when the *Venetia* was lost in 1868. He was a grandson of **David Gilbert** (1745-1821), master of the *Ceturah*.

David Owen Davies (1878-1964), Glenroy, Parrog Road, was master of the *Idomeneus* in 1940. He married Mary Anne (Polly), daughter of **John Hughes**, St Mary's Cottage.

David Phillips Davies (1856-1917), son of **John Davies** (1824-77), was second mate on the SS *Gisella* that was sunk by enemy action on 17 April 1917.

Enoch Davies (1838-79) was mate on the *Alfred* 1874-75 and then on the *Talca* on which he died at sea on 22 October 1879.

George Davies (1858-90) was mate on the *Hesper* from 1886 but nothing was heard of the vessel after 20 January 1890 and he was presumed drowned.

George Davies, apprentice, was lost at sea during the 1914-18 war.

George Davies, master of the *Ann & Mary* 30 tons at Newport in 1877.

Henry Davies, born in 1817, was master of the *Mariner* in 1858.

Isaac Davies (1804-56) was master of the *Duke of Cambridge* of Dublin in 1855.

James Davies* (1818-56), master of the brig *Culloden* 83 tons built at Newport in 1804, died suddenly at South Shields on 25 June 1856. By his wife, Mary, who kept the Ship Aground in Lower

Bridge Street, he had a son, **William Davies** (1837-1907), master mariner, and later proprietor of the Commercial (now Castle) Hotel.

James Davies (1859-1954), Llwynderw, East Street, sailed to the north Pacific in the 1880s and was master of the SS *Blodwen* at Bremerhaven in 1906. He was familiarly known as 'Cocky Bach' and his caricature appeared in a Matt cartoon of local celebrities in *The County Echo* on 21 November 1935.

Jenkin Davies was master and owner of the *Eagle* at Newport in 1876.

John Davies* (1766-1835), master mariner, was the son of Evan Davies, mariner, a native of Newport who had moved to Cardigan, by his wife, Mary Davies of Parcypratt. In 1785 he started a general merchants' business at Bridgend, Cardigan, with his elder brother, Thomas Davies, who also became a ship owner and a merchant banker. In 1789 he married Ann, daughter of Thomas Jones of Newport, where he settled and established himself as the leading merchant and ship owner in the history of the port (p. 9). He died in 1835 and he and his wife, and their son William, are commemorated in the chancel of St Mary's Church. By his wife, Ann, he had six sons and two daughters:

> **Llewelyn Davies** (1790-1819), master of the brig *Alliance* 126 tons built in Bideford in 1793 and used for conveying timber from Sweden until it was captured and set on fire by the American brig of war *Argus* in August 1813, of the sloop *Ecton* 55 tons in 1814 and of the snow *Albion* 166 tons built by his brother-in-law William Roberts of Hakin in 1815. On 21 May 1818 the *Albion*, set out from Caernarfon with eighty emigrants sailing to St John, New Brunswick. The next day, the master dropped anchor in Newport bay and went ashore and spent the night at home. A contemporary account, written on board, describes the scene:
>
>> At 1 p.m. we anchored off Newport in Pembrokeshire. We saw the white houses of the town, others scattered among the trees, the church tower tall and white, two high towers of the ruined castle: a pleasant site, the land looking green and promising. To the south, above the town, a fairly high mountain rose into a rocky head bare of everything except heather:

> south-east a high rocky steep, and beyond it, good land
> facing south: here and there a man sowing. All looking as if
> providence smiled on the land. . . . After anchoring the
> master went ashore to see his family, and some of the
> passengers to do their shopping. We were much stared at, a
> ship and a load of Welsh people about to leave their country
> and to face a long voyage to a far land. Many wished to join
> us, but the master forbade it. We got what we needed here
> and were shown much kindness and attention. We meant to
> take some beer with us, but it was very poor stuff.

The following day, the master returned with his father and
some of the sailors' wives who had come to wish the company a safe journey. The ship raised sail and anchor and a fair
wind soon took them past Strumble Head. Forty-five days
later, on 7 July, they anchored in Perth Harbour, Amboy, New
Jersey. The voyage is commemorated in a Welsh ballad, *Môr-
daith y brig Albion* (The Voyage of the brig Albion) and it
inspired the author Llywelyn Wyn Griffith to write his book
The Way Lies West.[22]

The vessel foundered on the Arklow Banks on 11 November
1819 with the loss of all hands. Llewelyn Davies had married in
1814, Mary, daughter of **Owen Harries** (1759-1828) by
whom he had two daughters, Elizabeth and Ann. In 1824 his
widow married his cousin, **William Davies** (1775-1865),
master of the *Eliza* of Newport, and had two sons, **Llewelyn
Davies** (1827-80), master of the *Defiance*, and **William
Davies*** (1829-56), master of the *Mary Ellen.*

Evan Davies (1794-1826), master of the *Mary & Eleanor*,
married Mary Harries of Fishguard where he settled and by
her he had two daughters, Anne and Martha. His widow
transferred the shares that she had received in the will of her
father-in-law to John George of St Dogmael's.

David Davies (1801-30), master of the schooner *Alert*, was
drowned off Brest.

John Davies* (1805-36), Cross House, was drowned when
the brig *Margaret* 128 tons, which had been launched only a
few months earlier at Milford, sank with all hands on 11 July
1836 on a voyage from the Baltic to London. By his wife,

Margaret Morgan, he had a son, Thomas, who was a master mariner, and a daughter Anne, who married **Thomas Rowlands** (1824-65).

Thomas Davies, born in 1807, vicar of Trevethin, Gwent.

William Davies (1810-39) had received in his father's will two storehouses, a coal house and a smithy on the Parrog and was expected to succeed his father as merchant and ship owner at Newport but he died four years later when he was only 29 years of age. His property was sold by public auction at Parrog and at the Commercial Hotel on 13 December 1839 and this marked the end of the brief period of prosperity of the Davies family at Newport.

Margaret Davies, born in 1796, married **William Roberts**, shipwright of Hakin, who built, among other vessels, the *Albion*, the *Hope* and the *Margaret*. After her husband's death she took charge of the 126 ton brig *Ant* of Milford which he had built for himself in 1816, until she sold it in 1847. They had a son, Thomas Roberts, JP, DL, of Hamilton House, Milford.

Anne Davies, born in 1804, married **David James**, master mariner, who was drowned off Milford in 1828 on the sloop *Elizabeth & Mary* built by the Havards at Newport in 1792, leaving a daughter, Anne, and a son, Thomas Davies James, who is commemorated on a tablet in St Mary's Church chancel as 'a young man of considerable promise as respects piety and attainment.'

John Davies (1800-69), master of the Newport built brig *Minerva* 102 tons from 1860 to 1869, died at Milford on 5 December 1869 and was buried at Ebenezer Independent Chapel.

John Davies (1814-60), was master of the *Crystal Palace* sailing to Kronstadt in 1856.

John Davies (1816-75), master of the *Diligence* from 1861 to 1874 and of the *Saladin* that sailed on 7 October 1875 but was not heard of again. He married Grace, daughter of **Llewelyn Griffiths** (1779-1866), master mariner, of the Ship Inn.

John Davies, Fountain Cottage, born in 1819, was mate on the *Orion* sailing to Balaklava in 1855, on the *Cape Range* to Malta in

1856 and on the *Xiphias* 1859-61 with **John Morris**, Ivy House, as master, to Bombay, and then on the *William Miles* in 1861, the *Queen of India* 1862-63, the *Ondara* 1866-67 to Quebec, the *Flying Cloud* that was lost on 29 December 1868, but he survived and served on the *Forest Queen* 1869-70 and the *Tryphena* in 1882.

John Davies, born in 1823, was mate on the *Ann* 1865-72, the *Midsummer* 1872-76 and the *Greta* 1877-81.

John Davies* (1824-77), mariner, of Parrog, was drowned off Milford on 25 August 1877 leaving three sons who lost their lives while at sea: **David Phillips Davies** (1856-1917), **Thomas Rees Davies** (1861-99), and **John Lloyd Davies** (1866-1923). A surviving son, Clement L. Davies (1870-1933), lived at Anchor House, West Street.

John Davies (1825-74), Penrallt, master of the *Forest King*, was drowned when the vessel was lost at sea on 19 March 1874. His daughter, Mary Anne, married Jesse Varney, six of whose seven sons were seafarers (p. 97).

John Davies (1838-84) was drowned when the *Condor* was wrecked in January 1884.

John Davies, an able-bodied seaman, was killed in action in the 1914-18 war.

John Davies* (1843-1923), served as mate on the *Globe* from 1867 to 1872. He was master of the *Bacchus* 1874-82 sailing to Rangoon and of the *Lord Cairns* 1882-1901 trading with Australia. He died on 11 March 1923 leaving by his wife, Margaret Jane, daughter of **David Thomas**, Fern Cottage, master mariner, three sons who were seafarers:

> **John (Johnny) Davies**, born in 1881, signed on as an apprentice on the full-rigged *Merioneth* of Liverpool on a voyage round Cape Horn to San Francisco. He was second mate on the *Loftindus* when it collided with the German ship *Corisande* and was one of only seven survivors landed by that ship at Pernambuco. During the 1914-18 war he served in the Royal Naval Reserve and was sent to the Mediterranean as an anti-submarine defence instructor. He was at Heligoland and received the Mons Star for his work on the Dover patrol. He commanded the *City of Poona* and the *Caernarvonshire* on

their last voyage to be broken up in Japan. Between 1924 and 1940 he was master of the *Pentaff*, *Dhandon*, *Acadialite*, *Otira*, *Drakedene*, *Charlwood*, *Arletta*, and of the *Stanwell* when it was struck by bombs and set on fire during the Spanish Civil War in an air raid off Tarragona on 16 March 1938, killing two of the crew and injuring four others. During the 1939-45 war he made four journeys to the Black Sea taking petrol to Romania. He was chief officer of the *Empire Construction* in 1947.

He is remembered as a man of few words and of bulldog appearance. When there was some dispute as to who had won a competition at the local regatta and the complainant said that he would 'refer the matter to the regatta committee,' Johnny swung round and yelled: 'I am the bloody committee,' and that put an end to the matter. Earlier that morning, whilst preparing for the regatta, he was standing on a rock with his back to the sea, pulling at a rope in order to secure the diving board, but the rope snapped and Johnny fell backwards into the sea. His tweed hat floated on the water for some time before he appeared like a great bull seal, but with his pipe still in his mouth. Nobody would dare laugh.

When Newport received its only royal personage with the visit of the Princess Marina, Duchess of Kent, in 1951, the mayor, appointed Johnny to be in charge of flags and bunting to decorate the town, and requested him to make sure that the Welsh flag would hang over The Square, where the royal car would come to a halt. When the mayor arrived in his robes, ready to receive Her Royal Highness, he saw, instead of the Welsh dragon, an enormous flag, one half of which was black and the other white, flying from the tops of telegraph poles and sweeping the ground. The mayor was furious and ventured to berate Johnny. He coolly explained that he had been unable to find a large Welsh flag and so he had rigged a flag indicating: 'Stop or I fire across your bows!' [23]

Herbert Davies (1885-1972), Castle Green, Dinas, was mate on the *Favonian* in 1909, the *King David* 1909-10, and the *King Lud* 1912-14 that was sunk in 1914 and the master, **David Harris** (1873-1954) and crew were taken prisoner. He was later master of the *King Malcolm* that was sunk on 7 February 1917 and he was taken prisoner near Alexandria and put aboard a submarine sailing through the Straits of Otranto into the Adriatic Sea, which had such trouble negotiating the wire netting defences placed by the Italians as an anti-submarine device, with water entering the submarine and the heat being unbearable, that its commander admitted that it was the worst experience of his life. He spent two years in captivity in Germany. He was master of the *King John* in 1919, of the *Apsley* 1919-21, and of the *King Edward*, *King Frederick* and *King Stephen* between 1921 and 1939. He died on 27 May 1972 and he and his wife, Margaret Elizabeth, are buried at Macpelah cemetery, Dinas.

David Reginald Davies (1893-1940) was married to Florence Davies of Netley Abbey, Hampshire, and died while serving as second engineer on the *Craigwen* of Cardiff on 9 October 1940.

John Davies, born in 1851, was mate on the *Kooringa* 1884-86 and on the *Aberystwyth Castle* in 1887.

John Davies, Castle Street, born in 1852, master of the *Charleston*, *Gloriana*, *Myra Fell*, *Snowdon Range*, *Malvern Range*, *Tamaqua* and the *Pinemore* between 1908 and 1923.

John Davies (1856-1916), master of the *Escurial* 1887-88 and of the *Marbella* in 1888, was drowned when his ship, the *Franz Fischer*, was destroyed by a bomb from a zeppelin off Kentish Knock on 1 February 1916.

John Davies, born in 1857, was mate on the *Florence Danvers* at Falmouth in 1881.

John Davies, master and owner of the 34 ton smack *Unity* at Newport in 1876.

John Davies, master of the smack *Favourite* at Newport in 1876.

John Davies, master of the 23 ton flat *Price Jones* at Newport in 1878.

John Lloyd Davies (1866-1923), son of **John Davies** (1824-77), died at Santa Fé on 18 July 1923 as the result of an accident sustained while serving as mate on the *Lundy Light*.

John Vaughan Davies, **BEM**, Spring Cottage, Dandre, went to sea as a deck boy bound for South America on the 9,000 ton cargo ship *West Wales* which was blown ashore in a gale and wrecked. He then served on the *Raseby* carrying sugar from Cuba that ran into a gale but the ship managed to limp into port. During the 1914-18 war he was quarter-master on the *Cliftonian* when it was sunk by a submarine in February 1917. In the following September he was torpedoed whilst on the *City of Lincoln*. From 1924 he was boatswain on the coaster *Goodig* which carried ammunition from the Bristol channel ports to Scapa Flow during the 1939-45 war. In 1946 he joined the *Struan* of Leith whale hunting in Antarctica and on the return journey, while bathing at Bahia Blanca, he was attacked by an octopus so severely that he was kept in hospital for several weeks, wrapped in cotton wool. He was awarded the British Empire Medal for his war service.

John William Davies* (1899-1917), son of David and Margaret Davies, Pant-teg, Long Street, was assistant cook on the SS *Torrington*. He died on 9 April 1917.

Joseph Davies (1868-1916), master mariner, of Llysfair, Upper St Mary Street, was drowned while serving on the SS *Bayreaulx* which was reported missing after leaving Cardiff on 20 October 1916. He married Jane Phillips and had a daughter and three sons, one of whom, **Alcwyn Davies**, was a master mariner.

Lewis Davies served at sea under Capt. John Isbester of the Shetland Islands whose daughter he married and lived at Peerie Hoose, Parrog. In 1908 he was presented with an inscribed watch by the mayor of Fremantle for his services in navigating for twenty-five days in an 18 foot open boat of the ship *Carnarvon Castle* that had been abandoned on fire at sea.

Llewellin Davies, born in 1847, was master of the *Rosy Morn* 1871-76 and of the *Mary Emily* 1876-78. On 8 June 1885, when he was master of the *Earl of Lonsdale*, the vessel was stranded at St Agnes, Scilly Isles, and he was found in default.

Llewelyn Davies (1827-80), son of **William Davies** (1775-1863), was master of the schooner *Defiance*.

Llewelyn Davies* (1832-1908), Cemaes House, was master of the brig *Crusader* 185 tons from 1876 to 1883. In 1877 he sailed from Lyttelton, the port of Canterbury, New Zealand, to London in the record time of 67 days.[24] As a reward for transporting the racehorse Perkin Warbeck to New Zealand its owners presented him with a travelling clock. He died on 2 November 1908, aged 76 years. He had married Mary, the eldest daughter of **David Havard** (1802-43), Cemaes House, by whom he had two daughters, Jane, who died in 1936, and Mary Davies, spinsters, of Spring Hill.

Morris Davies, Goat Street, born in 1832, was master of the *Victory* 1882-88 and of the *Cambrian* in 1888, sailing to the West Indies, Africa and South America.

Morris Davies, master and owner of the *Lerry* at Newport in 1879.

Samuel Davies, a boy of 13 years of age, was serving on the *Ann & Betsey* when he was drowned at Landshipping in 1861.

Thomas Davies, born *c.*1782, was an ordinary seaman serving on HMS *Dreadnought* at the battle of Trafalgar.

Thomas Davies, born in 1795, was master of the *Prince of Wales* 1856-62.

Thomas Davies, (1825-76), master of *Her Majesty* and of the *Lady Aberdour* sailing to the Mediterranean, died at Kustendje, Romania. He was a brother of **Benjamin Davies** (1831-87) and of **David Davies** of the *Amcott*.

Thomas Davies (1842-75) was mate on the *Magnet* when, on a voyage from Buenos Ayres to Mauritius in 1873, the vessel sprang a leak and foundered. He was then mate on the *Mary Frost* and was drowned on 11 July 1875 off Mossoro, Brazil.

Thomas Davies* (1866-99), Long Street, died in Rio de Janeiro.

Thomas Davies, born in 1897, the son of John Davies, Holmhouse Isaf, was mate on the SS *Framlingham* 1934-36, and on other vessels before he became a harbour pilot in Swansea, one of his pilot boats being the *Roger Beck*. He married Grace, granddaughter of **Thomas Beynon**, master of the *Merle*. His son, **John Beynon Davies**, was a mariner.

Thomas Davies, master of the 27 ton smack *Margaret Ellen* at Newport in 1877.

Thomas George Davies* (1901-37), son of David and Sarah Davies, Bentinck Terrace, was drowned at sea on 15 October 1937.

Thomas Rees Davies (1861-99), son of **John Davies** (1824-77) was found dead, possibly murdered, at North Towawanda, New York, on 9 August 1899.

Walter Davies (1832-83), Long Street, mate on the *Lillie*, died at Varna, on the Black Sea, on 17 February 1883.

Wilfred Eurfyl Davies, stoker, died on 7 October 1944 on H.M. Trawler *Vidonia* whilst on Royal Naval patrol service and was buried at Bayeux war cemetery.

William Davies* (1775-1863), West Street, was master of the snow *Eliza* of Cardigan 148 tons sailing to North America in 1818. The vessel was captured and taken to a French port where he and the crew were held prisoners. He married Mary, daughter of **Owen Harries**, master mariner, and widow of **Llewelyn Davies** (1790-1819) and had two sons, **Llewelyn Davies** (1827-80) and **William Davies*** (1829-56).

William Davies (1819-1903), master mariner, of Rock House in 1871, then of Dandre, and of Cambria by 1881, was master of the *City of Lincoln*, sailing from Cardiff to Ascension Island in 1857. On a return voyage from Quebec on 3 December 1860 the ship had to be abandoned and the crew of fifteen landed at Queenstown (Cork), with the exception of **John Francis**, boatswain, who was drowned. William Davies married Hannah, daughter of **Thomas Jenkins**, Spring Hill, master of the *Tit-bit*.

William Davies, born in 1821, was mate on the *True Blue* in 1858 and on the *Young Marquis* in 1871.

William Davies (1827-70), West Street, sailed as mate on the *Nell Gwyn* from Cardiff to Panama on 30 December 1868 but the vessel was not heard of after 7 February 1870 and he was presumed lost.

William Davies (1827-76), mate on *Sedwell Jane* 1875-76, died at Santos on 28 March 1876.

William Davies, born in 1828, was mate on the *Quickstep* in 1858.

William Davies* (1829-56), son of **William Davies** (1775-1863), was master of the schooner *Mary Ellen* that was lost with all hands in St George's Channel on 5 February 1856.

William Davies (1837-70), was master of the *Victory* from 1868 to 1873 sailing to India, and of the *Malleny* from 1873 to 1876 sailing to Singapore. He later lived at Bellevue, Dinas, and he and his wife, Elizabeth, were buried at Ramah cemetery, Dinas.

William Davies* (1837-1907), master mariner and, later, proprietor of the Commercial (now Castle) Hotel, from where ran *Y Shah* the daily coach to Crymych (p. 114). He was a magistrate, a prominent member of the Carningli Branch of the Ancient Order of Foresters, chairman of the St Dogmael's District Council, and, as mayor of Newport 1898-99, he 'originated the Town and Parrog Fund'. He married Mary, daughter of **John James** (1808-92), Westleigh. He later lived at Morawel, Parrog Road, which he and his wife gave to Bethlehem Baptist Chapel for use as a manse, for which purpose it was occupied for many years.

William Davies (1851-80), Lower St Mary Street, sailed as third mate on the *Agamemnon* from London to New Zealand in 1872 but the ship was wrecked and he was discharged on 11 September at Cape Town. He was master of the *Lilly Maud* that disappeared without trace in 1880.

William Ellis Davies* (1892-1943), quarter-master, died at sea through enemy action on 27 March 1943, leaving a wife, Jane Ellen, who died on 31 March 1952.

William Howell Selby Davies, son of Thomas John Selby Davies, Dolwerdd, went to sea in 1923 and was a mechanical engineer on fifteen ships including the *Vancouver City*, the *Taunton*, the *Dalmore*, the *Usk Valley* and the motor vessels *Camroux 3* and *Camroux 11* sailing to China, Japan, the Philippines and Australia. He served in the North Sea convoys during the 1939-45 war and escaped without injury when his ship struck an acoustic mine in the Thames in 1941. He settled at Tywyn, Meirionydd, where he celebrated his 100th birthday on 22 January 2005.

William Morgan Davies, born in 1857, was master of the *Garston* in 1887.

Joseph Dodding (1795-1864), master of the snow *Ardent* of Cardigan 125 tons from 1826 until the vessel was lost off the Shetland Islands on 11 January 1858, and then, from 1861 to 1863, of the sloop *Frances* 33 tons. 'Jo Dodin' is shown on an estate map of 1815 as tenant of a house in Upper St Mary Street, where his two spinster sisters lived at Scolton Lodge. The Doddings were active workers at Ebenezer Independent Chapel where a gravestone commemorates 'Joseph Dodding, who having led an active career as a seaman for upwards of 54 years, departed this life on March 3rd 1864, aged 69 years'. His daughter, Margaret Ann, married Daniel

Jones, headmaster of Talybont School, Ceredigion, and left £40 in her will to Ebenezer on condition that the family graves were maintained in good order.

Donald Edwards, **MBE**, was a chief radio officer employed by the Marconi International Marine Communication Co., Ltd. He went to sea in 1929 and served on a number of vessels, including the *Empire Purcell* that was sunk on 27 May 1942 and the *Empire Modred*, that was torpedoed during darkness on 8 February 1943. He succeeded in manning a lifeboat and took charge of the boat while the ship's master was incapacitated. He was appointed a Member of the Order of the British Empire for his gallant and meritorious services. He married Megan, daughter of David Thomas, Swnydon.

Oliver James Edwards (1903-41) lost his life on 3 April 1941 whilst serving as mate on the SS *Greenawn*.

Thomas Edwards, West View, master mariner, who died in 1918, had two sons who were mariners and two daughters, one of whom married a master mariner: **Thomas David Edwards** (1885-1945), like **George Adams**, had to take to the lifeboat when the SS *Ellington* foundered off the coast of Spain and row to the port of Vigo. He was master of the *Ocean Fame* when he died in 1945. **Allan Edwards**, born in 1889, was lost at sea. Elizabet Hannah, daughter, married **John Owens** (1880-1947).

Tom Edwards* (1897-1923), son of James Edwards, Upper Bridge Street, lost his life at sea on 27 October 1923.

William Edwards, Brondesbury House, Market Street, able seaman, lost his life while serving as a fireman on SS *Cressida* on 17 March 1918.

John Ellis (1811-68), Bryn-y-môr, Parrog, was mate on the *Symmetry* in 1860-61 and master of the *Northern Gourds* in 1867, when the ship was lost. He was then mate on the *Forest Queen* which was lost with all hands on 10 November 1868 sailing to the West Indies. He had two sons: **George Ellis**, who was drowned during the 1914-18 war, and **John Ellis**, mariner, who settled in Australia, and a daughter, Evangeline, who married **Thomas Lloyd Hughes**, marine engineer, son of **John Hughes** (1846-94), and lived at Bryn-y-môr.

William Ellis (1818-67), mate on the *Star of the North* in 1866-67 sailing to Bombay.

Arthur John Evans (1892-1933), son of the Rev. John Evans, vicar of Crickhowell, and his wife, Anne, who came to live at Spring Gardens. He married Anne, daughter of Dr David Havard by his wife Julia Anne, daughter of **John Rowlands** (1819-81) and was medical superintendent of the Elder Dempster Shipping Company. He was medical officer on the passenger ship *Port Kingston* which arrived at Kingston, Jamaica, on 14 January 1907 as the town was being destroyed by an earthquake, and he rendered surgical assistance to a large number of people. His account of the earthquake appeared in *The British Medical Journal*. In 1916 he served on HMHS *Oxfordshire* as part of the relief force following the fall of Kut but he was invalided home. He died in 1933 and his ashes were scattered on Carn Ingli.

Benjamin Roderick Evans of Pantyderi was the master of the *King Lud*, launched in 1928, that was torpedoed and sunk off the east coast of Africa by the Japanese on 8 August 1942 sailing from New York to Bombay with a cargo of government stores, when all hands were lost. His widow, Dr Rowland Evans, lived at Newport.

Daniel Evans (1767-1829) was master of the brig *Valiant* 117 tons built at Newport in 1812. He held shares in the *Albion*, **Llewellyn Davies** (1790-1819) master. In April 1825, the Court Leet gave him consent to build a quay from his 'New Quay unto John Jenkins's Quay.' He was mayor of Newport 1825-26. He married secondly, Grace Morgans. By his first wife, who died in 1803, he had a son, **Daniel Evans** (1801-77), Cwrt Bach, who was an apprentice at sea in 1812. He married Martha Devonald of nearby Blaenpant in 1827. He was mate on the *Malvinas* of Llanelli in 1851. In March 1877, he was master of the 15 ton smack *Miss Sarah*, belonging to **William Thomas**, that brought coal, culm and limestone regularly to Newport. The vessel arrived at Newport with a load of culm on the afternoon of 20 August 1877 at 4.15 p.m. and, after discharging, it departed on its next voyage and was lost with all hands off St Ann's Head on 25 August. He had a son and four daughters, one of whom, Grace, married **Thomas Beynon**, of the *Merle*. His son, **William Evans**, married Mary Morris of Mwnt in 1868 and worked as a rigger at Cardiff where he died in 1916.

David Evans (1798-1834), master of the schooner *Brothers* of Newport, was married to Margaret, daughter of David Harries.

David Evans, master and owner of the *Ellen* 26 tons at Newport in 1876.

David Evans, master and owner of the *Eliza Anne* 31 tons at Newport in 1878.

David Evans (1836-80), master of the *Sauvegarde* from 1875 to 1879, died of coast fever at Massabe, West Africa, on 14 April 1880. By his wife, Martha, he had a daughter, Elizabeth, who married **David Llewellyn** (1867-1933), Maesyrafon.

David Evans* (1838-1918), Spring Gardens, was master of the *Easternhill* from 1878 to 1886. He died on 31 October 1918.

David Evans, born in 1841, mate on the *Billow* was drowned when the vessel was lost on 28 January 1868.

David John Evans (1864-1900), Wellfield Grove, Parrog, master of the *Candida*, went to live in Birkenhead where he died on 2 January 1900. His daughter, Florence Kato Evans, returned to live at Newport and married **Thomas Gilbert Mathias**, master mariner. His brother, **Thomas Meyrick Evans**, was drowned off Pondicherry.

James Evans, master of the *Britannia*, owned by Ann Rowe, at Newport in 1876.

James Evans (1832-78), born at Newport, moved to Penmynydd, Dinas, and was master of the *Quadroon* 1868-74 and of the *Gertrude* which left Coosau River on 27 September 1878 and was lost with all hands.

James Evans, (1839-1915), born at Fishguard in 1876, lived in St Mary Street, and then at Bettws. He was master of the *WHB* of Swansea in the 1880s carrying copper ore from Chile to Swansea. He was buried at Nevern.

John Evans, born *c*.1781, served as an ordinary seaman on HMS *Britannia*.

John Evans (1795-1866) was mate on the *Symmetry* 1856-58. He died in April 1866 and was buried at Caersalem. He was the father of **Thomas Evans** (1826-1906).

John Evans, born in 1820, was mate on the *Uzella* in 1868, the *Sarah Ann Widdup* in 1877, the *Magnet* 1879-80 and on the *Syren* in 1883.

John Evans, born in 1822, was mate on the *Rhoda* of Milford at Newport in 1856.

John Evans (1835-98) was master of the *Cambay* from 1872 to 1876 sailing to the Americas, the *Canute* 1876-77 sailing to the East Indies, and of the *Stadacona* 1879-81. He was afterwards landlord of the Plough Inn, now Welford House, where he died in October 1898 and was buried at Ebenezer Independent Chapel. The inn was then kept by his daughter, Blanche Evans, a small timid lady who was a devout member of Ebenezer and, as the result of the religious fervour of the time and the drive towards temperance and, no doubt, the persuasion of her friends at the chapel, she surrendered the licence in 1904 and the inn was closed. Her action received wide publicity and acclaim in the local newspapers and she was held as an examplar to other publicans.

Llewelyn Evans was owner and master of the *Two Partners* which foundered in Lydstep Bay in 1762 and was plundered by five men from the neighbourhood.

Llewelyn Evans, born in 1838, was master of the *Star Queen* 1868-71 sailing to Brisbane, the *Cavour* 1872-4 to Rio de Janeiro and Bombay, and of the *Armathwaite* 1886-88 to the West Indies.

Owen Evans* (1787-1872) was master of the schooner *Martha* which was said to have been the last ship built on the Parrog (p. 22).

Raymond Evans (1899-1917), son of Benjamin R. Evans, Virginia House, West Street, was an apprentice on the *Paddington*. He died through enemy action on 21 July 1917.

Thomas Evans* (1772-1847), Goat Street, and later of Tower Hill, master mariner, died on 13 November 1847.

Thomas Evans, born in 1807, master of the *John* in 1859 and of the *Alfred & Emma* in 1862, was pensioned on 15 June 1864.

Thomas Evans (1820-66), son of William Evans, Quarrel, was master of the brig *Albion* 1859-62.

Thomas Evans (1826-1906) was born in Mill Lane and later lived at Sea View. He went to sea when he was twelve years of age as a cabin boy on the brig *Hinton* of Cork, of which his father, **John Evans** (1795-1866), was master. In 1850 he was admitted to the Pontypool Academy and, having decided to become a missionary, he was sent to India. In 1873 he and his family spent their summer holidays at Spring Gardens on a break from his missionary work In 1895 he came back to this country on account of his wife's illness and served as unordained minister at Bethlehem Baptist Chapel for a year before returning to India in 1898. He died in 1906 at Moradabad, Uttar Pradesh, and was buried there. His biography, *A Welshman in India*, was published in 1908.

Thomas Evans* (1851-1921), Glanafon, master mariner, was the son of David and Margaretta Evans of the Ship Inn, now Gwynfi House. He married Anne, daughter of David and Margaret Lewis of the Britannia Inn, next to the Llwyngwair Arms. He sailed to Yokohama in 1872 on the *Ivanhoe* and was master of the *Delano* 1892-94 sailing to the USA. His daughter, Irene, married **David Laugharne Havard** (1887-1953), marine engineer. **William Evans** (1849-89) was his brother.

Thomas Evans,* master mariner, married Ellen Elizabeth, daughter of the Rev. Llewelyn Lloyd Thomas, rector of Newport from 1824 to 1875. She later kept a school at Bwlchmawr, Dinas, with her two daughters, Elizabeth and Margaret.

Thomas George Evans* (1854-1933) was master of the *Mizpah* 500 tons. In September 1884 he sailed his ship through the 360 mile long Straits of Magellan, an achievement, it was said, 'that only one navigator of the seven seas can lay claim.' He was twenty-nine years of age and said that he had done so in order 'to save time, instead of rounding Cape Horn.' He was 'five days and five nights continuously on the bridge,' he recalled, and 'dropped anchor four or five times owing to bad weather, then, on the fifth day, I could see nothing other than being blown on the rocks, but just at the crucial moment, when disaster seemed imminent, the wind veered in the right direction enabling me to get clear.' Whenever his name was mentioned, people would add *sotto voce*: 'His hair turmed white in one night,' but he rather spoiled the story by stating: 'My hair turned grey in a single night with the strain and anxiety.' After he retired, he was largely instrumental in having the Memorial Hall built of stone and mortar, rather than of corrugated zinc with a stone façade, as originally planned, and he suggested the provision of a Reading Room as part of the hall 'where the young people of the town could spend their leisure hours, instead of going to public houses,' for which he contributed £100 together with a further £20 towards its furnishing, in memory of his wife, Mary Elizabeth. This was agreed and work commenced on 1 January 1922 and the Hall was opened on 26 September 1923. The Reading Room, regrettably, was never equipped for this purpose and was simply furnished with a large book case with a few, mostly unsuitable, books and a table and chairs, but it developed as a source of information for the towns-people who had a connection with the sea. A copy of the *Western Mail* was provided daily and laid out on a table in the middle of the room and secured to the table with a thin brass bar so that the paper could not be removed. It was invariably open at the page in which there was a column headed 'The Movements of Vessels' and it was here that those who had kinsfolk on the sea could discover their location.

Thomas Meyrick Evans,* mariner, son of John and Anne Evans of Wellfield Grove, and brother of **David John Evans** (1864-1900), was drowned off Pondicherry, on the Coromandel coast of India, aged 21 years.

William Evans, born in 1809, was master of the *Mary* of Milford in 1856.

William Evans, Quarrel, master of the brig *Vine*, was drowned with all the crew on a voyage from Galway to London in March 1837. By his wife, Elizabeth, who later lived at Fountain Hill, he had a son, **Thomas Evans** (1820-66), master of the *Albion*.

William Evans (1830-1907), Cross House, master mariner, was the son of Benjamin Evans of Parcymarriage Farm. He was master of the *Mary Jane* 1862-68. He was said to have been a pioneer in gold mining in California which enabled him to retire early from the sea. He bought Cross House in 1867 and had it rebuilt, and he and his wife lived there for the next forty years during which he ran a coal and culm merchant's business. He was mayor 1878-80 and a member of the Penybont Bridge Committee 1891-94. He was a deacon and treasurer and occasional precentor at Ebenezer Independent Chapel and he supported Capel-y-Mynydd, a branch of Ebenezer, near Parcymarriage. He died on 1 December 1907 and was buried at Ebenezer.

William Evans (1849-89), West Street, was the son of David and Margaretta Evans of the Ship Inn, and a brother of **Thomas Evans**, Glanafon. He served on the *Malleny* 1873-81 sailing to Rangoon and the East Indies, and was master of the *Curlew* 1882-85 and of the *Bacchus* 1886-8. He died at Falmouth on 3 September 1889.

William Eynon* (1823-75), a native of Fishguard, master mariner, lived at Spring Hill and died at Bonny River on the west coast of Africa on 27 September 1875.

Frederick W. T. Farr* (1867-1921), master mariner, born in Woburn in 1867, married Caroline, daughter of **Thomas Griffiths**, master mariner, of Cnwce Farm. They lived at College Square before moving to St Rest on the Parrog where he died on 19 November 1921.

Henry Rees Felix, marine engineer, was born in Cardigan in 1860. He lived at Bridge House next to which was the Post Office, now the Library, where he was the postmaster until he retired in 1902. He was a magistrate and chairman of the bench for a number of years, and mayor in 1904-06.

David Francis* (1812-80) was master of the *Lively Lass* in 1861 on a voyage to Barbados, and of the *Fanny* 1867-79 sailing to Smyrna. He was married to Margaret, daughter of William Daniel of Panteg, Eglwyswrw. He died on 7 June 1880 in New York.

John Francis (1825-60), boatswain on the *City of Lincoln*, **William Davies** (1819-1903) master, was washed overboard and drowned when the ship was abandoned at sea on 3 December 1860.

Benjamin William George* DSO (1885-1958), son of **Thomas George** (1840-1902) by his wife, Margaret Evans of Nevern. He ran away to sea and sailed as an apprentice on the *Merioneth*, celebrating his fourteenth birthday off Cape Horn on the way to San Francisco. As master of the *Tredegar Hall* he succeeded in beating off a German submarine after a four hour engagement on 17 July 1917 for which he was awarded the Distinguished Service Order. He received Lloyd's Silver Medal for meritorious service and the Gold Medal of the Shipping Federation for recovering an abandoned vessel. After the war he served with Gibbs of Cardiff on the *East Wales* and on the *West Wales*. Commander RNR. He died on 27 February 1958. He married Annie Jane Havard, daughter of John Havard, ironmonger, and lived at Greenacre, Long Street. He had two seafaring sons: **William Havard George** who had a distinctive career during the 1939-45 war in that he was, at first, a chaplain in the Royal Navy, then an officer serving in the Royal Marine Commando, and finally an Army chaplain, and **John Thomas Havard George**, a pilot at Swansea who married Peggy Owen, a grand-daughter of **David Owen**, master mariner, Grove Park.

David George, son of Owen and Catherine George, was an ordinary seaman on HMS *Amethyst*.

John George, born in 1840, sailed on the *Arbitrator* 1873-76 to New Orleans, Pernambuco and Bombay until the ship foundered on 23 August 1876. He was master of the *Alice* 1878-81 and of the *Athabasca* 1883-88.

Levi George (1838-91) was master of the *Enterprise* when the vessel caught fire at sea and he was discharged at St Helena in 1869. He was master of the *Leon Crespo* which also caught fire at sea in 1882 and he was discharged in the Falkland Islands. He was later master of the *Mary Jose* 1885-88 sailing to the south Pacific. He was living at Swansea in 1876 and died on 12 April 1891 and was buried at Church Park, Glamorgan.

Stephen George (1845-82) was mate and, later, master of the *Acadia* which was lost at Ducies Island in the South Pacific on 5 June 1881. He was mate on the *Escambia* and was drowned when the vessel was wrecked at San Francisco on 19 June 1882.

William George, King Street, born in 1843, was shipwrecked on three occasions, the last being on the *Ethelwolf* when the vessel foundered near Vigo on 10 December 1886.

William George was master of the 23 ton smack *Sarah Ann* at Newport in 1885.

David Gilbert* (1745-1821), master of the brig *Ceturah*, is described on his gravestone as master of 'the first brig built at this port' (p. 19). By his wife, Ceturah, he had a son **David Gilbert*** (1790-1852), master of the *John* of Cardigan 1845-46 and 1851-53.

David Gilbert (1856-78), mariner, son of Thomas Gilbert of the Prince of Wales Inn now Llysmeddyg, by his wife, Eleanor (née Salmon). He died at Port Elizabeth at the age of 22 years.

David Gilbert (1874-94) was lost at sea in January 1894.

John Salmon Gilbert (1862-97), mariner, son of Thomas Gilbert of the Prince of Wales Inn, died of yellow fever on the barque *Lucia* in making passage from Aspinwall (now Cólon, Panama) to Satilla River on 5 July 1897.

William H Godfree (1854-88), coast guard, was drowned in Newport Bay on 17 November 1888.

Llewellyn Griffith* (1829-50), son of Llewellyn and Mary Griffith, Fern Hill, was drowned at sea near Dublin on 18 December 1850. He was a brother of **Thomas Griffith** (1824-63).

Benjamin Rees Griffiths, born in 1868, was master of the *Astracana* from 1896 to 1902 and of the *Maskinonge* 1912-21 which was involved in a collision with a vessel at anchor that sank on the St Lawrence river.

David Griffiths* (1789-1821) was master of the sloop *Darling* that sank with all hands on a voyage from Swansea to Newport on 9 October 1821.

David Griffiths* (1800-71) was master of the Newport-built schooner *Claudia* 135 tons from 1861 to 1867 and, in 1868, and later of the schooner *Harmony* 95 tons. He lived in West Street, next to the Plough Inn. He had two seagoing sons: **John Griffiths** (1827-1868) and **Thomas Griffiths** (1833-88), both of whom died unmarried, and two daughters, Elizabeth, who married **John Thomas** (1825-59), and Margaret whose sweetheart was drowned at sea and she remained unmarried.

David Griffiths* (1801-35) was master of the brig *Neptune* of Milford that was lost at sea off Milford on 10 October 1835 with all hands, including the master's wife who was on board.

David Griffiths* (1804-73), Penwern, master mariner, who died on 16 February 1873, had two sons who were master mariners. **Thomas Griffiths** (1830-74) and **David Griffiths** (1838-68).

David Griffiths, born in 1830, was mate on the *Jane* of Milford in 1856.

David Griffiths* (1838-68), son of **David Griffiths** (1804-73), was mate on the *Victory* in 1867 sailing to Calcutta and later master of the *William Wright*. He married Sarah Hughes, daughter of the Royal Oak Inn, and lived in West Street, but died at Penwern.

David Owen Griffiths, Trennydd, was born at Ystrad, Rhondda, and came to Newport as a boy. He was apprenticed in 1927 at Haines of St Ives and served on the *Trecarrell* in 1933 sailing to Vancouver, and he was mate on the *Trevorian* and the *Trelosck* sailing to the River Plate and to Canada. He was on the *Empire Stream* in 1941 when the vessel was lost through enemy action while in convoy to Gibraltar. He then served on the British Rail Fishguard-Rosslare ferry *St Andrew* which had been converted into a hospital ship and saw action at Salerno and at Anzio, where the ship helped to rescue survivors of her torpedoed sister hospital ship, the *St David*. **Cecil Joy** master. In 1942 the *St Andrew* struck a mine in the Adriatic, a few hours after General Montgomery had been on board, and she was towed back to Taranto by HMS *Wilton*. He was chief officer of the Channel Islands mail boat *Samba* which was the first to re-enter the islands after the war. He returned to the Fishguard-Rosslare ferry service and was master of the *St Julian* and of other British Rail vessels until he retired in 1977 as commodore of the Sealink fleet and marine superintendent at Fishguard harbour. He lived at Goodwick and died in 1988 and was buried at Manorowen.

Edward Griffiths, born in 1855, was mate on the *Sarah* 1882-83 and was discharged at New York on 5 July 1883.

Ellis Griffiths was master of the *John & Elizabeth* at Newport in 1876.

George Griffiths, Eastfield, Parrog, was a marine engineer. He married Leila, daughter of **Edward Richards** of 1 Mount Terrace. His brother, **William (Willie) Griffiths**, was also a marine engineer.

Griffith Griffiths, born in 1821, was mate on the *Isabel* when he was drowned on 12 November 1864.

Griffith Llewellyn Griffiths (1793-1846), master mariner, died on board the *Neptune* on 6 May 1846.

John Griffiths (1827-1868), son of **David Griffiths** (1800-71), was master of the *Ocean Queen* in 1860 and of the *Charlotte Harrison* in 1861-63, making voyages to Quebec, and of the *Ottila* 1865-66.

John Griffiths (1841-65), son of Thomas Griffiths of Bridge End, Newport, was mate on the *Mary* when he was drowned in the Bay of Biscay on 25 September 1865.

John Griffiths* (1843-56), son of David Griffiths of the Salutation Inn and formerly of Holmhouse Fawr, was drowned at Morwellian, Devon, on 3 June 1856 and buried at Tavistock. He was a brother of **Joshua Griffiths** and of **William Griffiths** (1835-53).

Joshua Griffiths (1832-77), Holmhouse Fawr, was mate on the *Mornington* 1869-73 and master of the *J. E. Millidge*, 1876-77. He died of a fit of apoplexy at sea in the roadstead of Garrucha, Spain, on 25 March 1877.

Levi Griffiths (1839-1907), master mariner, served on the *Floris* sailing to Nassau when the ship was lost on 6 May 1864. He was mate on several other ships until 1868 when he sailed to India on the *Walsgrif*. He was described in the 1901 census as a retired pilot, Port Louis, Mauritius. He built a pair of houses on Cotham Hill which he called Mauritius, afterwards renamed Bryn and Hafan. He was mayor of Newport 1899-1901.

Llewelyn Griffiths* (1779-1866), 'of the Ship Inn', was owner and master of the *Diligence*. His daughter, Grace, married **John Davies** (1816-75).

Llewelyn Griffiths (1854-75), son of **Thomas Griffiths** (1825-63), mariner, died at Portland, USA, on 30 January 1875.

Llewhelin Griffiths, master mariner, married Ann James and had a daughter, Frances, who married the Rev. John Davies (1810-80), minister of Gideon Independent Chapel, Dinas, and had seven daughters, one of whom, Frances, married **William Richards**, master mariner.

Samuel Griffiths, born in 1838, was mate on the *Edith* 1872-77 and the *Blanche* 1882-87.

Samuel Griffiths, master of the *Mary Ann*, was in difficulties off Aber Mawr in May 1906 and was rescued by the Fishguard lifeboat.

Thomas Griffith (1824-63), son of Llewellyn and Mary Griffith, Fern Hill, lost his life at sea in October 1863.

Thomas Griffiths* (1825-63), master of the *Triton* of Cardigan in 1858 and then of the *Mary Ann Hewitt* which sailed on 22 August 1863 and was not heard of again. By his wife, Mary, he had two sons **Thomas D Griffiths** (1853-77), and **Llewelyn Griffiths** (1854-75).

Thomas Griffiths (1825-89) was mate on the *Maggie* in 1876-77, the *WHB* in 1887 and on the *Albert* that was lost on 26 November 1889 and he was drowned.

Thomas Griffiths* (1830-74), Parrog, was mate on the *Trinity Yacht* of Liverpool 1856-57, *Nereid* 1857, *Horatio* 1857-58, *Ondara* 1858-60, and the *Forester* 1861. He was master of the *Ondara* 1862-65, *Economist* 1865-67, *Bessie* 1868-70, and of the barque *Royal Diadem* of Milford 1872-74. He died at sea off Mauritius on 21 January 1874 having made his will at Cape Town, probate of which was granted on 19 June 1874 to his widow and sole executrix. He was married to Hannah Jane, daughter of **Benjamin Thomas**, by whom he had a daughter, Mary Anne, who married **John Richards** (1845-1906).

Thomas Griffiths (1833-88), West Street, son of **David Griffiths** (1800-71), was master of the *Braemar* 1868-72, of the *Ilione* 1873-80 sailing to the Far East, and mate on the *Edinburgh* in 1880.

Thomas Griffiths* master mariner, described on his gravestone as 'Thomas Griffiths, master mariner, of Ship in this town,' may have been landlord of the Ship Inn, whose wife, Mary (née Hughes), died in 1875 aged 41 years.

Thomas Griffiths* (1840-85) of Tycanol Farm, and later of Cnwce, was master of the *Ocean Gem* that went ashore at Bic, on the St Lawrence river, in 1872, and of the *Glee Maiden* 1879-80 sailing to Batavia. Two of his daughters married master mariners: Caroline who married Capt. **Frederick Farr**, and Clare Nore, wife of **Edward Richards**, marine engineer. A third was the mother of **Eric Daniel**.

Thomas Griffiths (1877-1921), Tyrhos, near Brithdir, was master of the *Kamouraska* from 1916 to 1920. He died of Bright's Disease in August 1821.

Thomas Griffiths, born in 1880, was master of the *Llongwen* that was sunk by enemy action in 1916, but he was active at sea until 1945.

Thomas D. Griffiths* (1853-77), son of **Thomas Griffiths** (1825-63), was mate on the *Cardiganshire* and was drowned at Calcutta on 6 December 1877.

William Griffiths (1806-63) was mate on the *Jessie Miller* that foundered and he was discharged at St John's on 9 January 1861. He was then master of the *Duke of Cornwall* of which nothing was heard after 16 September 1863.

William Griffiths, born in 1898, was master of the *Iolo* that was sunk by enemy action on 20 February 1917 and he was taken prisoner of war and detained at Brandenburg. Between 1919 and 1925 he was successively master of the *Bradford City*, the *Jersey City* and of the *Leeds City*, that struck a reef near Bawean Island and sank on 20 September 1925.

William Griffiths* (1835-53), son of David Griffiths of the Salutation Inn and formerly of Holmhouse Fawr, died in Australia on 1 April 1853 and was buried 'in Bendigo Gold Diggings'. He was a brother of **Joshua Griffiths** and **John Griffiths** (1843-56).

William (Willie) Griffiths, East field, brother of **George Griffiths**, was a marine engineer.

John Grono (1767-1847), pioneer fur seal hunter and shipbuilder in Australia, was undoubtedly the most widely known of Newport mariners (p. 111).

Joseph Gronow (1825-84), Goat Street, mariner, died on 27 November 1884 aged 59 years.

William Gronow (1861-86), son of Stephen Gronow, Quarrel, Brynberian, was drowned on the island of Nodnail, Holland, on 17 November 1886.

Benjamin Harries, a native of Dinas who married Bessie, daughter of Caleb Morris, Tan-y-bryn, went to sea as an apprentice in 1912, when he was 12 years of age, on the *Daldorch* of Glasgow. During the 1914-18 war he was third mate on the *Dalblair* carrying munitions to Gallipoli. In 1920 his ship, the *Mercuria*, was frozen in sea ice off Estonia. He obtained his master's certificate in 1923 and served on the Red Star Line of passenger ships. He devised and patented *The Harries Course & Bearing Indicator*, 'a novel instrument . . . permitting immediate indication of direction to be read without ambiguity.' (*The Journal of the Institute of Navigation*, January 1956).

David Harries was the owner of the Newport built sloop *Flora* 28 tons and of the brig *Charlotte* 81 tons.

Howard Levi Harries (1915-40) was the eldest of three sons of Thomas Harries the blacksmith, whose smithy was opposite Ebenezer Chapel, to be drowned at sea when their vessels were attacked by German submatrines during the 1939-45 war. He was chief steward on the *British Monarch* that was sunk on 19th June 1940 by the U-48 with the loss of the crew of 40 men. **David Glyn Harries**, third officer on the *Empire Stream*, was drowned on 25 September 1941 aged 25 years, when the ship was sunk by the U-124. **Kenneth George Harries**, third engineer on the SS *Garlinge*, was drowned on 10 November 1942, aged 21 years, when the vessel was sunk by the U-81. **Harry Leonard Harries**, another brother, who was at sea from 1936 on the *PLM 13* was excused further sea duty in December 1942.

James Harries (1837-75) was second mate on the *Coromandel* that sailed from London for Bombay on 19 April 1875 but was not heard of after 30 June that year and he was presumed drowned.

Levi Harries, master and owner of the *Penelope* 27 tons at Newport in 1878.

Owen Harries (1759-1828), master mariner, of Pendre, bequeathed his estate, including land called Rangland that lay to the west of Newport Castle, to his wife. He owned shares in the brigs *Sampson*, *William*, *Eliza* and *Artuose*, the sloop *Trident* and the schooner *Eliza*. By his wife, Elizabeth, he had two seagoing sons and a daughter: **Thomas Harries*** (1788-1855) of Pendre, master of the *Sampson*, was mayor in 1843-45. He was mayor of Newport 1843-45. He died on 2 February 1855 and was buried with his wife, Mary, who had died in 1834, aged 41 years, on the birth of her thirteenth child. **William Harries*** (1798-1846), master mariner. Mary, his daughter, married, firstly, **Llewelyn Davies** (1790-1819) master of the *Albion* and, secondly, **William Davies** (1775-1863) and by him had two sons, **Llewelyn Davies** (1827-80) and **William Davies** (1829-56), both master mariners.

David Harris* (1873-1954), Oakfield, Castle Street, married firstly Letitia Evans, daughter of John Evans of the Royal Oak and secondly, Hannah Isaac. He served with the Court and King Lines and was master of the *H. H. Asquith* and of the *King Lud* which was captured in the Indian Ocean in 1914 by Seine Majestat's Schiffe *Emden*, one of the most notorious German raiders of the war. The master and crew, which included **Herbert Davies** and **Thomas Gilbert Mathias** from Newport, were ordered off the ship before it was sunk and were taken to Colombo and held as prisoners-of-war. Under its master, Karl von Müller, the vessel wreaked havoc in the Indian Ocean, where it intercepted 32 Allied vessels and sank 18 British ships and captured three colliers loaded with coal. The *Emden* was eventually destroyed in a running battle with HMAS *Sydney* off the Cocos Island. Capt. Harris was master of the *Margam Abbey* in 1917 when the vessel was torpedoed and beached near Philippeville, and of the *David Lloyd George* from 1922 to 1927. A later *King Lud*, launched in 1928, was torpedoed by the Japanese and sunk with the loss of all hands in 1942, under the command of **Benjamin Roderick Evans**.

David Havard (1731-1817), son of Owen Havard, carpenter and farmer of Pendre Farm, succeeded his father at Pendre until 1814 when he surrendered the lease and moved to Dandre. He is the first shipbuilder of whom there is an account at Newport, and the founder of a ship-building family that built more than forty vessels in their yard on Parrog (p. 19). He married Jane Thomas and died in 1817 leaving a son, **John Havard*** (1771-1839) who married, firstly, his cousin Mary Phillips of Cnwce who died in 1814 and, secondly, in 1825, Margaret George (1780-1852), of the Ship Afloat, now Seagull Cottage, a widow. His death was reported at the Court Leet held on 25 October 1839 and he is commemorated on his gravestone at St Mary's churchyard as a shipbuilder. By his first wife he had four sons and three daughters, who married master mariners:

> **David Havard*** (1802-43), master mariner, Cemaes House, West Street, who married Phebe, daughter of **Thomas Nicholas** (1747-1843), Mount Pleasant, master mariner. He was master of the brig *Phebe* 125 tons, built by the family in 1839, and named after his wife, which was lost with all hands in a storm. Lloyd's reported from Aberdovey that 'a vessel is sunk about 3 miles to the northwards with 2 masts above water. Some papers have been picked up near the spot marked "Capt. David Havard *Phebe* of Newport, Pembroke-shire."' His daughter, Mary, married **Llewelyn Davies** (1832-1908), master mariner.

> **William Havard*** (1804-53), master mariner, married Anne, also a daughter of **Thomas Nicholas**, Mount Pleasant, in 1840. He was master of the brig *Anne* 161 tons built at Newport by Levi Havard in 1842. He died on board ship at Limerick on 3 December 1853 His wife had predeceased him on 22 April 1845 giving birth to their son, **David Havard** (1845-1919) who was brought up by his widowed aunts Phebe Havard and Mary Davies. At the age of fifteen he wanted to go to sea but, in view of the loss at sea of no less than five members of the family, endeavours were made to prevent him and his uncle, **David Nicholas**, master of the brig *Excel*, was asked to take him with him and to give him a rough time so as to dissuade him from seeking a seafaring career. In this he succeeded for the boy broke ship at London and came home overland. In time, he qualified as a doctor and practised at Newport. He married Julia Anne, daughter of **John Rowlands** (1819-81) and had a son, David Havard (1884-1956), medical practitioner and magistrate at Newport.

Levi Havard (1812-81), Dandre, shipbuilder. In 1847, as he could see that the larger vessels soon to be in demand could not be floated across the bar at Newport, he transferred the shipbuilding business to Castle Pill, Milford, where he remained until he retired in 1859 and returned to Newport to live with his widowed sister, Mary Davies, at Dandre. He died unmarried on 28 October 1881 and his obituary stated that he 'gave employment to hundreds of his townspeople' in Newport and that his 'well known face and kindly advice will be missed by many.'

John Havard (1814-49) was master of the family-built schooner *Claudia* 103 tons in 1835 and is believed to have been at sea when he died of 'cramp in the bowels.' He was unmarried.

Elizabeth Havard married Llywelyn Jenkins, master mariner.

Anne Havard (1798-1819) married **Rowland Rowlands** (1793-1852), master mariner and had a son, **John Rowlands** (1819-81).

Mary Havard married **David Davies** (1815-55), master mariner. She kept the family papers which have been deposited at the National Library of Wales.

David Havard, born in 1835, younger son of Levi Havard, ironmonger and a distant cousin of **David Havard** (1802-43), obtained his master's certificate in 1862. He was mate on the *Caroline* in 1876 and on the *Doris* sailing to Sydney where he was discharged in September 1883. He married Martha, daughter of William Mathias in 1871 and lived on Parrog Road and had:

Levi Havard, born in 1862, mariner, who married and settled at Barry and left no issue.

William Havard (1865-1938), master mariner, Bank Terrace, who is shown on the 1881 census as a mariner living at Pendre with his widowed mother, Martha Havard, grocer, and his sister, Frances, and brother, John (1872-99). He was mate on the *Prince Sottykoff* in 1887. He married Elizabeth Anne Thomas and had a son, Jack Havard, mariner, and a daughter,

Bessie, who married **Redouin Lewis Vaughan James**, marine engineer.

John Havard (1833-1924), elder son of Levi Havard, ironmonger, was mate on the *Liffey* in 1861-62. He married Elizabeth Llewellyn and gave up the sea to succeed his father as an ironmonger. He had four sons and a daughter, who all had a seafaring connection:

> **Essex Harries Havard**, born 1880, Lieutenant Royal Navy.

> **David Laugharne Havard*** (1887-1953), ship's engineer with Furness Withy of Cardiff. He married Irene, daughter of **Thomas Evans**, Glanafon, master mariner, and was church warden at St Mary's church from 1943 until he died.

> **Thomas Norman Havard*** (1891-1925), master of the *Afon Lliedi* 1922-25 and of the *Derville* that left St. Anthony, Newfoundland, on 15 October 1925 for Malaga and was lost with all hands.

> John Llewellyn Havard succeeded his father as ironmonger, and was followed by his son, **Essex Havard**, who went to sea as an ordinary seaman in 1940 on the *Temple Pier*, **Howard Phillips** master, that was captured by the French at Algiers in July 1940 (p. 66). From August 1942 to August 1943 he was third radio officer on the *Empire Breeze* that was torpedoed by an U-boat in the north Atlantic and the survivors were abandoned on rafts. He then served on the *Kaimata* and on the *Highland Chieftain* until the end of the war. He was founder of the Newport Surf Saving Club and was a county councillor. He died in 1999.

> Annie Jane Havard married **Benjamin W. George**, DSO.

John Havard (1871-99), mate on the *Oberon*, was drowned when the ship was reported missing on 26 January 1899.

Owen Havard, born *c*.1750, went to sea when he was fifteen years of age and followed the coastal trade for twenty-one years. He was master of the sloop *Little Hetty* that belonged to George Bowen of Llwyngwair. He made an application for charity to Trinity House on 8 June 1820 on behalf of himself and his wife, Lettice. The application was certified by the churhwardens who stated that the Register of Charities had been lost but that they believed that Owen Havard was 70 years of age.

David Higgon, born in 1836, was mate on the *Coils* and was discharged at Yokohama on 7 April 1869.

William (Willie) George Hogan, Heathfield, Upper St Mary Street, born in 1892, was master of the *Skegness* of the William Reardon Smith Line.

William Hoskins* (1874-1955), born at Porteynon, Gower, master of the SS *Abermaed*, married Margaret Anne, daughter of **David John** (1822-76).

John Howell, born in 1820, was master of the *Armistice* 1860-66 sailing to Spain and Portugal.

Thomas Howell, seaman, lost his life at sea during the 1914-18 war.

Dewi Howells, mariner, son of Thomas Howells and his wife, Florence (née Hogan), of Heathfield, Upper St Mary Street, lost his life on the *Norman Monarch* during the 1939-45 war.

Freddie Howells, son of Howell Howells, died on 29 March 1918 while serving as cook on the *T. R. Thompson*.

Benjamin Hughes, born in 1837, was mate on the *Douglas Castle* in 1869.

David Hughes, master of the *Ivanhoe*, alleged ill treatment by **Abel Rees**, a member of the crew, who faced charges that were partially proved at a naval court at Callao on 4 February 1876.

Eynon Hughes, born in 1809, was mate on the *Essequebo* 1859-60 and master of the *Emma* 1868-70 and of the *James Stewart* 1871-72.

John Hughes, Penrhiw Fach, born in 1837, served as mate on the *Sierra Madrona*, the *Alicar* and the *County of Anglesea* between 1882 and 1899.

John Hughes, born in 1837, was mate on the *Sea Foam* 1883-84 and on the *Ellen Catherine* 1887-88 and, as master mariner, he sailed to San Francisco, New York and Calcutta.

John Hughes, born in 1843, was master of the *Statesman* 1877-81, of the *Historian* 1882-87 and of the *Merton Hall* 1888.

John Hughes* (1846-94), St Mary's Cottage, now Lluest, master of the *Montgomeryshire*, was awarded a silver medal by the Norwegian Government for rescuing the crew of the *Otterea* of Norway in December 1886. He was master of the *Afon Cefni* that was lost at sea with a crew of seven men, all from Newport, in January 1894. By his wife Mary (née Lloyd), he had three sons who were at sea, and two daughters who married seafarers:

> **Thomas Lloyd Hughes**, born in 1876, marine engineer, who married Evangeline, daughter of **John Ellis**, master mariner, Bryn-y-môr, Parrog.
>
> **John Gwilym Hughes**, marine engineer, who was married and settled in Australia.
>
> **George Hughes** (1884-1917), second-engineer, who lost his life at sea through enemy action on 11 August 1917.
>
> Alice, the elder daughter, who was the organist at St Mary's Church, married **William Owen Williams**, master of the *Penolver*, and Mary Anne (Polly), who married **David Owen Davies**, Glenroy.

Thomas Hughes, born in 1834, was master of the *Baltic* 1868-71, the *Cornucopia* 1878-80 and of the *Arbitrator* in 1881.

William Hughes (1837-73) was mate on the *Thornhill* sailing from Liverpool to Quebec when the ship was lost on 15 November 1873 and he was drowned.

David Isaac, born in 1821, was mate on the *Bonito* in 1875 and on the *Duleep Singhi* in 1879 in the East India trade.

David Isaac (1843-86) was mate, and then master, of the *Sylhet* 1873-84 and master of the *Allahabad* which was last heard of on 4 September 1886. He had three sons who were master mariners: **Joseph Isaac*** (1870-1927), **William Isaac*** (1880-1949), and **David Isaac**, born in 1882.

David Isaac, born in 1882, master mariner, married Margaret Owen of the Barley Mow and had a son, Idris Isaac, who lost his life in the Far East during the 1939-45 war.

James Thomas Isaac (1880-1959) served at sea as a ship's carpenter. He was the last heard by the author to sing the ballad to *Y Shah* (p. 114). His son, **George Isaac**, (1903-87), Bridge House, was steward on the *East Wales* and on the *West Wales* sailing from Cardiff.

John Isaac* (1832-89) sailed as mate on the *Lotus* 1869-70 and was on the *Amethyst* when he died at Galatz on 17 April 1889.

John Isaac (1839-88), West End, mate on *L'Esperance* 1882-88 sailing to the Cape, died on 13 July 1888.

John Isaac, born in 1880, was master of the *Admiral Codrington* in 1919.

Joseph Isaac* (1870-1927), 3 Mount Pleasant Terrace, son of **David Isaac** (1843-86), died in hospital at St Vincent on 12 September 1927. He was married to Elizabeth Mary, daughter of **John Mathias** and had two daughters, one of whom, Irene, married **George Thomas**, master mariner.

William Isaac, born in 1828, was mate on the *Miranda* 1855-56 and on the *Prospero* 1856-58 sailing to St John's, the *Franby* 1858-59 to Valparaiso, on the *Culloden* to Aden where he was discharged in 1860, on the *Floating Light* 1860-62 and the *Galineau* 1863-64 to Bombay. In 1864 he sailed in the *Faside* to join a ship being built at Miramichi, New Brunswick. He was master of the *Sandringham* in 1864 and of the *Silvia* in 1881.

William Isaac* (1880-1949), Gwylfa, Upper Bridge Street, son of **David Isaac** (1843-86) master mariner, with whom a number of young men of the town did their apprenticeship. His daughter, Violet Isaac, married **Roachie Thomas**, marine engineer.

Thomas Peter Jacob, born in 1810, was mate on the *William & Sarah* in 1874.

Daniel James (1838-73), master of the *Thornhill*, lost his life in the Quebec River on 15 October 1873.

Daniel James, Coedfryn and his brother, **Jack James**, were mariners.

David James* (1770-1851), Dandre, master of the *Princess Royal*, by his wife, Ann, had two seagoing sons: **George James** (1801-71) who had the brig *Adroit* of Cardigan built for him by Levi Havard in 1845, and **David James** (1805-27), master of the *Princess Royal*.

David James, (1815-70), master of the *Sarah Anne*, was drowned on 11 May 1870.

David James (1818-60), master of the *Forest Queen* in 1858, was discharged on 9 October 1860 at Rio de Janeiro, where he died a fortnight later.

David James (1832-84), was master of the snow *Triton* of Cardigan from 1872 to 1874 when the vessel was abandoned off the Scilly Isles. This was one of three occasions on which he had to abandon ship in the Atlantic Ocean. He was master of the *Dillwyn* 1879-81 sailing to South America, and of the *Elephant* which was lost with all hands in 1884.

David James* (1842-1912) was master of the *Auburn* from 1868 to 1872 sailing to Japan and Sri Lanka, and of the *British Princess* from 1880 to 1905 sailing to the Americas. According to the 1881 census, the ship was docked at Liverpool and he had with him on board his wife, Elizabeth Anne (1886-1924), and daughters, Maud, who later lived at Bryncoed, Market Street, and Edith May, widow of the Rev. William Davies, later living at Hill Park, where she died on 23 September 1952.

David James* (1844-86), Tycoch, was mate on the *Star of Teign* which caught fire on 12 April 1867, and master of the *GBS* 1876-79 and of the *Agra* at Milford in 1881. He died at Penang on 6 January 1886. By his wife Margaret (1848-1931) he had **John Picton James*** (1865-1926), master mariner, and **David James*** (1874-94), drowned at sea in January 1894 aged 19 years.

David James (1864-1906) was mate on the *Oakville* when he died at Bilbao hospital on 30 November 1906 from injuries caused by falling from the rail.

David James, master of the sloop *Elizabeth & Mary* 60 tons, was married to Anne, daughter of **John Davies** (1766-1835) and was drowned when the vessel sank in Milford Haven in 1828.

Evan James was master of the *Gloucester Packet* owned by Mary James at Newport in 1877.

George James, born in 1849, was mate on the *Maggie* in 1879 when the vessel foundered, of the *Annie* 1892-93 and the *Primrose* in 1912.

Haydn James, son of Willie James, carpenter, Mill Lane, was at sea during the 1939-45 war and served on two vessels that were sunk by enemy action. His brother, **Hywel James** (1916-86), was on a ship that sank the day after peace was declared.

Jenkin James was master of the 27 ton smack *Farmer's Lass* at Newport in 1878.

John James, born in 1796, was master of the *New Harmony* from 1855 to 1858.

John James* (1805-68), West End, master of the brig *Felicity* of Milford, died at Cardiff on 25 February 1868.

John James* (1807-1902), Westleigh, was master of the *Robertson* 1856-66 and of the *Victoria* 1867-71. He was pensioned in 1872 and after he retired he became a wine and spirits merchant trading from his home. By his wife Mary he had three daughters who married master mariners: Mary married **William Davies**, (1837-1907) of the Commercial (now Castle) Hotel and later of Morawel; Emma lived at Westleigh after marrying **Albert Bowen** (1850-1902), and Elizabeth married **Frederick Seaborne** (1831-88).

John James (1811-37), master of the *Lady Day* of Milford, died at Cardiff on 5 February 1837.

John James, born in 1818, was master of the *Affigo* in 1865, of the *Gem* that was lost in West Africa in 1869, of the *Athole* that was wrecked on 2 October 1873 at Maio, Cape Verde, of the *Wexford* in 1874, and of the *Robert* in the same year.

John Pryse James, Pleasant View, born in 1867 at Trehaidd, Brynberian, was master of the *Nicaraguan* in 1903 and then of the *Cana* sailing to the South Pacific. By his wife, Mary Anne, daughter of **John Vaughan** of the Rising Sun, he had a son, **Redouin Lewis Vaughan James**, marine engineer.

Llewelyn James was mate on the *Gyon Castle* 1860-61 and on the *Mary* 1871-72.

Llywelyn James served as boatswain on the *Donald McKay* of which **James Price** was master.

Llewelyn James, born in 1820, was master of the *Orpheus* that was lost on 19 July 1860, and of the *Trent* that was stranded on a reef while trying to pass between Inagua Island in the Bahamas and St Domingo at night on 15 August, for which he was censured. He was master of the *Duke of Northumberland* from 1876 to 1880 and was awarded a silver medal by the Italian Government for rescuing, and conveying to Madeira, the shipwrecked crew of the *Fernando Po* which had foundered on 23 January 1879. He died at Spring Hill, Dinas, and was buried at Macpelah cemetery.

Redouin Lewis Vaughan James, marine engineer, was married to Bessie, daughter of **William Havard**, Bank Terrace.

Thomas James (1854-1918) was master of several Hall vessels and commodore with Radcliffes at Cardiff. His brother, **John James** (1864-1890), master mariner, settled in Australia where he was master of the *Kent* of Melbourne and was drowned when the vessel was lost with all hands in Green River.

Plan of Newport Bay & Harbour by Lewis Morris, 1748.

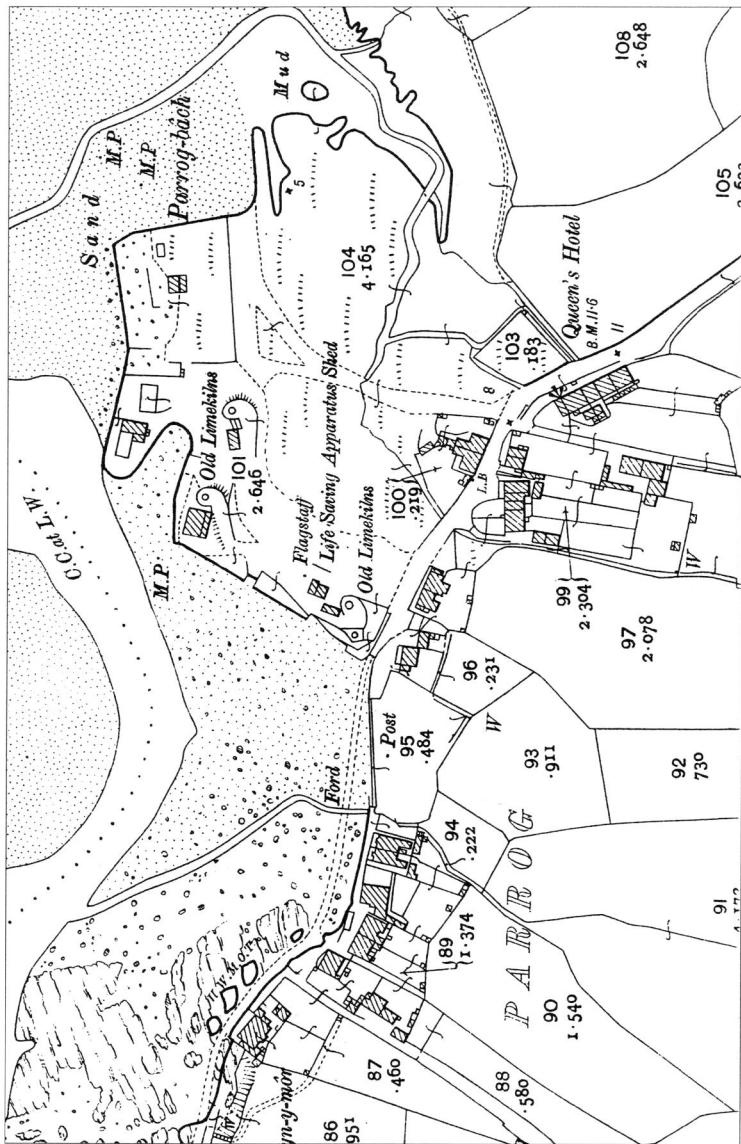

Plan of Parrog showing limekilns and storehouse sites (OS 1908).

Parrog from the east at high tide.
(By kind permission of Michael Simpson).

Parrog Bach with Havard storehouse.
(By kind permission of Michael Simpson).

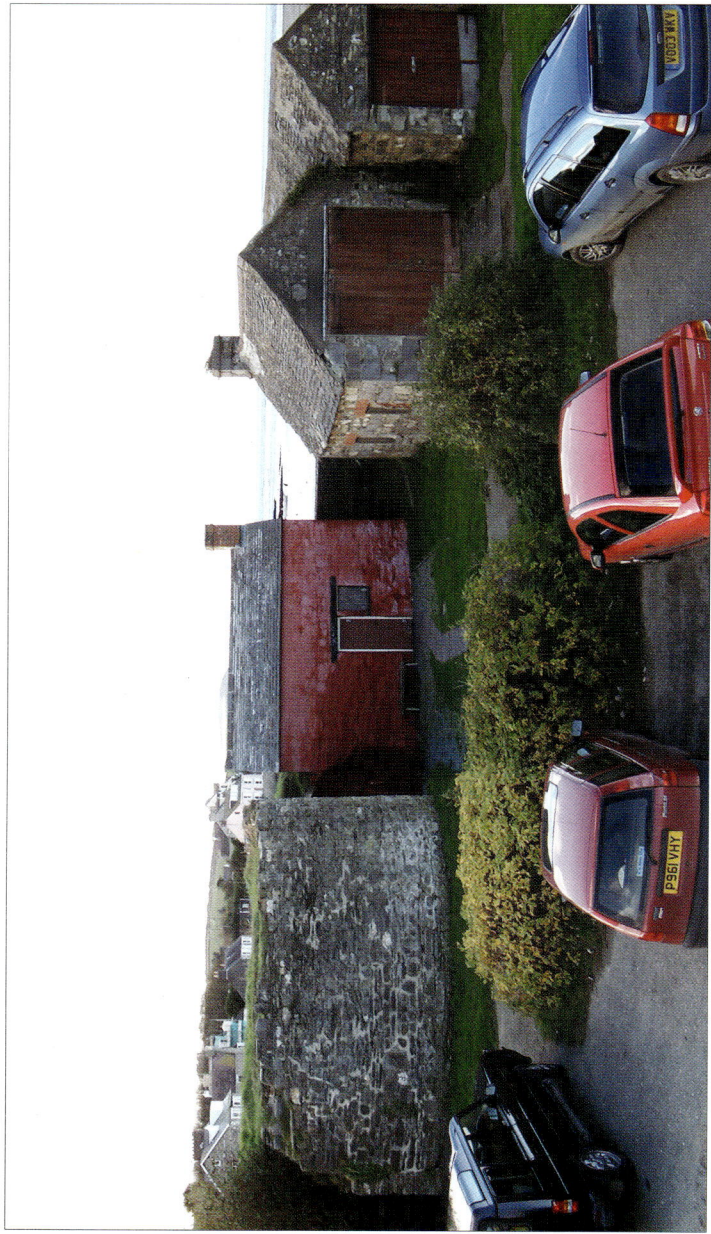

Lime burner's cottage standing between the surviving limekiln and Rocket Apparatus cart-house and mortuary. (By kind permission of Anthony Miles).

Sailors-to-be.
Ward Richards, John Vaughan Davies, BEM, and David Reginald Davies.
(Kindly loaned by Martin Lewis).

Jacob Beer directing repairs on the schooner *New Providence*,
31 tons, beached at Penybont, *c.*1885.
(By kind permission of Dr John Beer).

The dandy *Newland* 28 tons unloading at the quay wall behind Camelot.
Parrog Bach storehouse on left and Griffiths Trewern's storehouse
on right that was taken down in 1922 to provide stone to
build the Memorial Hall. Ferryman in foreground.
(By kind permission of Dr John Beer).

The schooner *Gleaner* of Cardigan, 1847.
(By kind permission of Dr John Beer).

Schooner beached on Chain Ford, probably while making for the quay wall behind Camelot, as horses and carts had to cross to Traeth Mawr to await their turn and then stand in the river to be loaded.

(By kind permission of John Ll. Havard).

SS *Harparees* 161 tons wooden screw barge built at Sittingbourne in 1920, one of the last ships to visit Newport, wrecked in 1929. (By kind permission of John Ll. Havard).

William James (1843-1903) was master of the brigantine *Tit Bit*, built at Bridport, from 1868 to 1871 and of the *Caranjah* in 1878, and mate on the *Ossian* 1886-88 sailing to the East Indies. He was a member of the Penybont Bridge Committee in 1891. He married Margaret, daughter of David and Margaret Lewis of the Ship and Castle, and was known for many years as 'Captain James the Ship'.

William James, born in 1857, was awarded a binocular glass by the French Government whilst master of the *Urbino* for services to the shipwrecked crew of the barque *Perigny* on 12 February 1897. He was master of the *Tampico* when it had to be abandoned at sea on 25 October 1907, and of the *Ripon*, *Grantford* and *Savannah* between 1908 and 1910.

Daniel Jenkins, born in 1801, was master of the *Brothers* in 1861.

David Jenkins* (1811-71) of Parrog was master of the 20 ton smack *Elizabeth & Mary* of Newport. While bringing a cargo of culm from Hook to Newport on 14 February 1861, the vessel was wrecked off Strumble Head. A boy was swept overboard but the master and mate were able to clamber on to a rock and were rescued by David Beddoe, sailor, and Albert Furlong, of the Great Western Hotel, Fishguard. He was also master and owner, of the sloop-rigged flat *Price Jones* 23 tons built at Flint in 1859 which he sold to **Thomas Roach** of Parrog.

Gabriel Jenkins* (1822-73), of Treffynnon, was mate on the *Laura* of Guernsey in 1851, on the *Fasfero* of Liverpool in 1853 sailing to Valparaiso and on the *Robert Barbour* of Liverpool to Calcutta in 1855. He was master of the 23 ton smack *Fly* of Newport from 1868 until it foundered near Newport on 24 April 1873 and he and his son, **Charles**, aged 15 years, were drowned. **David Nicholas** (1803-77), with whom he had sailed on the *Ocean*, feelingly recorded in his journal the 'sad and melancholy news of Capt. Gabriel Jenkins [was brought] by Capt. J.J. who saw the vessel's foundering.' He noted, on 14 July, that 'the smack *Fly* was removed to Cardigan for repair.' Another son, **David Jenkins**, mariner, lived at Channel View.

Henry Jenkins (1874-93) was drowned at sea after falling 'fore Royal Yard' while serving as ordinary seaman on the *Lord Cairns* on 19 June 1893.

John Jenkins, born in 1827, was master of the *Charlotte Harrison* in 1874 when the vessel was sailing to Quebec with a cargo of coal and iron and was wrecked at Blue Point, Aspy Bay, Cape North, but the crew was saved. He was master of the *Zimi* from 1876 to 1883.

Noyon Jenkins (1915-88), son of Charles Jenkins, Channel View, was a ship's carpenter on the *Temple Pier* when it was captured at Algiers on 3 July 1940. The master, **Howard Phillips**, and the crew, that also included **Essex Havard**, **Roderick Varney**, **Llewelyn Thomas** and his son, **Myrddin Thomas**, from Newport, were captured and taken prisoner and held at Camp Carnot at the foot of the Atlas Mountains until they were repatriated some six months later from Casablanca. Noyon Jenkins compiled 'a short historical account of our interment in a North African prison camp' in which he recorded that the vessel sailed from Cardiff to Milford Haven on 30 May 1940 and onward on 4 June in a convoy of sixty ships with destroyers and planes as escort, arriving at Gibraltar on 12 June. The vessel left Gibraltar on the 14th for Oran and, two days later, received orders to proceed to Algiers where it arrived on the 17th. 'We had discharged half our cargo of patent fuel,' he wrote, 'when we received orders from the British Consul to up anchor and clear out immediately. This was at four in the morning but no-one seemed to take notice of anything, so it was six a.m. before the night watchman came along aft to call us out to get the beams and hatches on also to lower the derricks. We worked like hell and had all complete by nine a.m. It was then that the Skipper told us that we couldn't get out as they [the French] had taken his clearance papers away. This was after the fall of France. A few days later, July 3rd, the day Oran was bombarded by the British Navy, we got taken ashore. We saw a tug coming alongside with French marines on board with fixed bayonets. They told us that we had ten minutes to get off the ship. We gathered together what we could. Most of my clothes were out on a line having just been washed: that was the last I ever saw of them. They chased the Skipper off the bridge with a revolver in his side. He only had a pair of slippers on and a jacket over his arm. Twenty minutes after, we were in jail!' Following the fall of France, the war cabinet had decided to put the French fleet out of action, which Churchill regarded as 'a hateful decision, the most unnatural and painful in which I have ever been associated.' The main force at Mer-el-Kebir (Oran), had refused to surrender and Admiral Sir James Somerville reluctantly carried out his orders and destroyed two battleships and a battle cruiser with considerable loss of life.

Samuel Jenkins, master of the *Ann & Betsey* at Newport in 1876.

Thomas Jenkins, Spring Hill, born in 1825, was master from 1868 to 1877 of the brigantine *Tit-bit* 133 tons built at Bridport in 1849. He was a deacon at Ebenezer Independent Chapel. His daughter, Elizabeth, married William R. Davies, Cambria Terrace, son of **William Davies** (1819-1903).

William Thomas Jermain (1839-1921) was born at Haverfordwest and brought to Newport when he was three years of age by his mother, and lived at Glanafon. He served his apprenticeship on the brig *Sophia* and then on the *Ondara* under **Thomas Williams** (1812-69) and afterwards served on the *Harmony*, the *Alma* and the *Symmetry* as sailing master. He was master of the *Madawasca*, the *Venetia*, carrying guano from the Chincha Islands and of the *Bacchus* sailing to the Far East. He married Jane, daughter of **David Nicholas** (1803-77), Mount Pleasant, and built the three houses known as Mount Pleasant Terrace on the site of two old cottages in 1894-95.

David John (1822-76), Pleasant View, son of **John John**, Alltclydach, and brother of **John John**, master of the *Orkney Lass*, and of **Morris John**, was mate on the *Jane Morrison* of which **John Morris**, Ivy House, was master, that was wrecked at Balaklava in March 1856 during the Crimean War. In 1857 he was master of the. *Express* of Liverpool and then of the *Georgiana* of Milford sailing to Quebec and of the *Hellespont* that sailed from Newcastle-upon-Tyne on 1 October 1867 to the Dardanelles, taking his family with him. They settled at Constantinople where he was master of the tug *Surprise*. On 14 October 1876, while towing a Greek vessel, he was swept overboard and drowned and was buried in the British cemetery in the Dardanelles. He had married his cousin, Elizabeth Ellen (née Thomas) who, after his death, returned to Newport and built a house in Market Street which she called Hellespont House. He left a son and two daughters, who married master mariners: **John Thomas John** (1855-1933), master of the tug *Los Santos*, working on the

Panama Canal from where he wrote a letter to his son, David Ambrose John, MM, on 13 November 1913, giving an account of his father's death and some family history. He died at Glendower, Dinas, on 17 August 1933. Mary married **John Vaughan** (1836-1908) of the Rising Sun, and Margaret Anne married **William Hoskins**.

Evan John* (1818-1892), Penrallt Fach, was master of the *Havelock* 1858-67 and afterwards of the smack *David* 26 tons, the 22 ton smack *Ann & Betsey* and of **Thomas Roach's** flat, the *Price Jones*. He died on 22 June 1892 leaving his wife, Sarah and a son, Thomas, who died at Penrallt Fach in 1928.

John John, born in 1823, was mate on the *Anne Wilson* 1863-65 and on the *Admiral Blake* in 1870.

John John, born in 1855, was master of the *Harold* in 1887.

John John, son of John John, Alltclydach, and a brother of **David John** and **Morris John** was master of the *Orkney Lass* bound for the East Indies when it sank off Brest.

John George John (1883-1916) was drowned while serving as mate on the *Mina Brea* on 28 June 1916.

Morris John, born in 1833, was a brother of **David John** and **John John** (1822-76). He was master of the *Rosalie* 1875-76, the *Belle* 1878-81 that was wrecked at St Anna, Gulf of Mexico, in 1881 and of the *Utopia* in 1888 sailing to the West Indies. He settled at Baglan Villa, Briton Ferry.

Henry Johns was master and owner of the *Rose* at Newport in 1879.

David Jones (1832-86), son of **William Jones** (1803-47), was master of the *Orso* from 1858 to 1864 sailing to New Orleans, Quebec, Sydney, and Bombay, and mate on the *Berbice* 1870, the *Athole* 1872, the *Clyde* 1873 that foundered off Valentia in 1876 and on the *Lord Macduff* that was lost with all hands on 19 October 1886.

David Jones, born in 1844, was mate on the *Enfield* when the vessel was wrecked in 1868 and later master of the *Dilawar* in 1884.

David Jones, Ivy House, master mariner, son of John and Eleanor Jones, Tycornel, was a deacon at Ebenezer Independent Chapel where his wife, Margaret Frances, daughter of **John Morris**, Ivy House, was active as a Sunday School teacher and promoter of temperance. He was mayor of Newport 1908-10.

Evan Jones, master and owner of the *Gloucester Packet* at Newport in April 1876.

Frederick Seaborne Jones, born in 1866, a grandson of **Frederick Seaborne** (1789-1851), was master of the *Roman* in 1886 at Bengal.

Gilbert Jones (1834-61), mate on the *Latona*, died at Calcutta on 8 May 1861.

John Jones* (1835-1923), Parrog, master mariner, married Anne, daughter of Thomas and Jane Hughes, Long Street.

John Jones (1871-1918), master of the *Commonwealth* that was sunk by enemy action on 21 February 1918.

John Jones, master and owner of the *Martha Jane* 17 tons at Newport in 1878.

Levi Jones (1797-1888), master of the *Pilot* of Milford, was drowned when the ship was lost on 25 October 1859.

Llewelyn Jones (1852-88) was mate on the *Santa Rosa* 1881 and on the *Regal* when he died at sea on 6 October 1888.

Peter Jones (1817-58), mariner, by his wife, Amelia, had a son, **Thomas Jones** (1844-65), mariner, who died on passage from Barbados to London on 14 May 1865

Richmond Jones, Tabernacle Cottage, was steward on the *West Wales* and the *East Wales* of which **Morris John Morgan** was master.

Robert Jones, born in 1830, was mate on the *Janet Wilson* that foundered on 27 March 1858 at Trieste, on the *Lancashire Witch* 1862-65 sailing to South America, and on *Her Majesty* that was lost in 1867 and, among others, on the *Norseman* 1871-75 and 1878-81 and the *Caldbeck* 1887.

William Jones* (1803-47) was master of the brig *Mary & Margaret* of Milford. By his wife, Mary Ann, he had a son, **David Jones** (1832-86).

William Jones (1839-64) was mate on the *Bessie Thompson* which sailed from Swansea on 8 September 1864 but nothing was heard of the ship after 1 December and he was presumed drowned.

Cecil Joy (1896-1979), a native of Weymouth, was on the *Arros Castle* when it was torpedoed 300 miles off the coast of Ireland during the 1914-18 war, and on the *Carlisle Castle* when it was torpedoed off Beachy Head. At the outbreak of the 1939-45 war he was master of the *St David* on the Fishguard-Rosslare Cross-Channel Line which had been commandeered as a hospital ship. The vessel sailed from Dover to Dunkirk on two occasions and, while they saw sixteen ships being sunk around them, they returned on both occasions with wounded and survivors to this country. Captain Joy's official report on the expedition of 24-25 May 1940 is as follows:

Sailed from Southampton for Dover, arrived 4.30 p.m., received orders to anchor, then cancelled, wait, at 7.30 p.m. received orders to anchor in Downs and return at 4.30 a.m. (25th) for orders. Received orders 6.30 a.m. to proceed to Dunkirk in company with SS *Worthing*. Course required passing over several patches of water 2-3 fathoms (Channel from Calais to Dunkirk being mined, had to pass around buoys to South'ward of same). Dead slow in wake of *Worthing* (drawing 11 feet) under heavy aerial attack and gunfire from Gravelines, proceeded into Dunkirk but no sign of life, did not know what berth to take, thought Germans were in occupation. Vessel stuck on mud in middle of harbour (Chart shows 18 feet), remained about one hour under aerial attack – swung ship and berthed between two wrecks. SS *Worthing* berthed astern of wreck during slight respite in attack. Several rumours of Germans in the town during our stay alongside but owing to intermittent aerial attack disregarded them. *Worthing* left (5-7 p.m.) agreeing to wait outside but owing to violent aerial attack he made off. We left 7 p.m. and were in addition to aerial attack, fired on off Gravelines. Several buoys missing, probably shot away as we were nearly hit on three occasions. Off Sandgattes the passage S. of Buoy was being covered by gunfire. I hauled across N. of the Buoy crossing 3 fathoms patch when I saw a shell hit the water about half a ship length ahead. Proceeded to Dover for orders then Newhaven Saturday midnight. Orders Sunday to return to Dover for orders. The Captain of SS *Worthing* protested about being under gunfire off Calais and asked for Northerly passage, so did I. Off Dover we dodged a mine and reported it. Anchored in Downs until Tuesday 2.45 p.m., several air raids during this time. Sailed on Northerly passage to Dunkirk. Heavy rain, poor visibility, followed route until nearly in when Destroyer warned 'Wreck ahead'. Went full astern and pulled up instantaneously as only dead slow. This passage meant passing over several patches 2½ fathoms. Echo sounder very busy.

Approached Dunkirk and lay alongside Causeway 7 p.m. until 7.30 a.m. Wednesday. During the whole night severe air attack and gunfire but not hit. Chief Engineer reported feeling touching something 3 p.m. on passage, deepwater must have been submerged wreckage or something? Also stayed in Dunkirk 2 hours alongside Causeway – rumour again, Germans in town. Standing by with axes to cut adrift, knocked down cement rails and rigged up gangway of funnel boards. During night vessel ranging against Causeway in swell, damage to belting, any other damage unknown. Several naval ships collided with port side, damage unknown – notably *Geraldbald*. Saw this vessel sail and sink outside harbour.

Sailed 7.30 a.m. behind *Prague*, dead slow over mines and shallow patches. Arrived Dover, ordered for Newhaven. STO asked "Is ship sea-worthy?" I said "Yes, she's gone to Dunkirk and back, some 200 miles since touching wreckage." Ordered diver inspection. Diver reported OK. Soundings all dry and fresh water in double bottom pure. So concluded OK.[25]

He modestly added: 'Carried some hundreds of wounded on both trips.' In fact, more than nine hundred persons were rescued.

The *St David* was sunk by the Germans off Anzio beachhead on 24 January 1944 and the *St Andrew*, that happened to be close by, was able to rescue survivors. Wynford Vaughan-Thomas, who was a war correspondent at the beachhead, observed in his book *Anzio*, that it was 'difficult to excuse their sinking of the British Hospital ship *St David* in the early days of the landing, because the *St David* was brightly lit according to the International Red Cross Code and she was illuminated in accordance with the terms of the Geneva Convention.' Cecil Joy retired from active service in 1943 on account of poor health. He married Joyce, daughter of E. M. Davies, Llysmeddyg, and joied in her enterprise as a market gardener.

Thomas Lamb, master of the 25 ton smack *Mountain Maid* at Newport in 1883.

William Lamb, master of the 25 ton smack *William & Maria* at Newport in 1883.

William Laugharne, born in 1821, was master of the *Bedford* in 1866 and of the *Esther* in 1883.

Cecil Lewis (1907-42), master mariner, son of Thomas and Anne Lewis, Upper St Mary Street, died at sea on 16 March 1942 while serving as chief officer on the *Stangarth* leaving a wife, Harriet, living at Endon, Staffordshire.

David Lewis (1838-72), master mariner, son of **Thomas Lewis**, mariner, was drowned when the *James Marychurch* was wrecked in 1872.

David Lewis (1858-1904) serving on the *Kingfisher* fell overboard in Poole Quay on the night of 13 October 1904 and was drowned.

David Lewis (1872-1923) of Craig-y-môr was master of the *Nairn* which was torpedoed on 27 August 1917 by the raider *Dresden* between Malta and Port Said with no loss of life. He died at Tampico, Mexico, on 3 October 1923 while serving as chief officer on the *Tecumseh*. By his wife, Ida (née Roach), he had four sons who were at sea: **Glyn Lewis**, mariner, **Gerald Lewis**, mariner, **James (Jimmy) Lewis**, marine telegraph operator, and **John Archibald (Archie) Lewis*** (1905-83), master mariner, of Hilston, who joined the *W. I. Ratcliffe* in 1921 sailing to Montreal. During the last war he served on ships of the King Line ferrying munitions and supplies, and was on the *King Edwin* in a North Atlantic convoy when more than a third of the vessels in the convoy were lost. In April 1943 he was on the *King Edwin* carrying a load of high octane petrol when it blew up in Valetta harbour. After forty-four years' service at sea, he was made a Commodore of the King Line.

David Lewis, master and owner of the *John George* at Newport in 1880.

John Lewis, son of **Thomas Lewis**, mariner, was mate on the *Economist*, **Joshua Nicholas** *master*, when he was drowned on 12 December 1874.

John Lewis, born in 1848, was mate on the *Ophelia* 1876-77 and on the *William Davies* 1881-83, and master of the *Honderklip* 1883-85.

John Lewis, mariner, died at sea on 2 December 1886 aged 17 years.

John Lewis went to sea when he was 12 years old in 1794. He served on the *Eliza* in 1818 sailing to Quebec and was lost on the *Ant* on voyage from Limerick to Glasgow in 1830.

John Evans Lewis (1865-1925), mate on the *Ely Rise* 1886-68, died at Cardiff on 21 March 1925.

Morris Lewis of Tyrhibyn, born in 1878, served with the Elder Dempster Line and was torpedoed three times during the 1914-18 war and as many times during the 1939-45 war.

Stephen Lewis, master of the *Phoenix* 23 tons, in 1876.

Thomas Lewis, mariner, had two sons who lost their lives at sea: **David Lewis** (1838-72), and **John Lewis**, drowned on 12 December 1874.

Thomas Lewis, born in 1836, was master of the *Sarah* 1878-84 and of the *Emma* in 1888.

Thomas Lewis, born in 1852, was mate on the SS *Abermaed* in 1886-88 and afterwards on the SS *Abertawe*.

William Lewis* (1804-33), Dandre, master of the schooner *Eliza*, died on 29 June 1833.

David Llewellyn, Long Street, born in 1825, was master of the *Sarah Ann* 1869-76, of the *Cornucopia* that was wrecked in 1880 and of the *Superior* 1884-86.

David Llewellyn (1867-1918), Maesyrafon, Upper St Mary Street, served on the *Escrick* when it was sunk by enemy action on 16 August 1918 and he was drowned. He married Elizabeth, daughter of **David Evans** (1836-80), master mariner.

Thomas Llewellyn* (1837-73) lost his life in the North Sea in November 1873.

David Llewhelin (1812-71), son of David and Maria Llewhelin of Forest Farm, was master of the schooner *Maria Eliza* 97 tons built at Cardigan in 1841 and of the *Canmore* 1857-61 sailing to Quebec. When he left the sea he became a farmer and settled at Maesgwynne Farm, Fishguard, where he died in 1871. His brother, **Titus Llewhelin** (1823-58), master of the *Sarah* in 1857 and of the *Catherine Jane* of Milford in 1858, died in London and was buried at Macpelah cemetery, Dinas.

William Llewhellin, mariner, of Penybont, died in July 1843 leaving everything to his wife, Mariah, who died on 19 September 1864. Her will was proved by **William Davies** (1819-1903) of Quay House, Parrog, master mariner, nephew of the deceased and sole executor.

Stephen Llewhellyn (1843-70), mate on the *Semiramis* sailing from Cardiff to Galatz, was drowned at sea on 22 March 1870.

David Lloyd, West Street, went to sea in 1791 when he was 15 years of age and served on ships for 56 years, latterly as cook and seaman on the *Pembroke Castle* of Milford sailing to Quebec.

David Lloyd (1847-80), West Street, was second mate on the barque *Agamemnon* sailing in 1872 from London to Canterbury, New Zealand, on which **William Williams**, Westfa, was the first mate, and **William Davies** (1851-80) the third mate, when the vessel foundered in Table Bay, Cape Town, on 7 September 1872. He was master of the *Chrysolite* 1875-77 and mate on the *Zelica* of which nothing was heard after 1 October 1880 and he was presumed drowned.

Eynon Lloyd, shipwright, built the sloop *Mary* in 1819.

James Lloyd, born in 1824, was mate on the *Excel* of Milford in 1855.

John Lloyd, born in 1824, was mate on the *Pink* 1857-51, the *St Aubin* 1877-84, and the *William Cory* in 1885.

John Lloyd* (1824-66), master mariner, was lost at sea in November 1866. He left two sons, **Llewelyn Lloyd*** (1853-76), who was drowned at sea in October 1876, and **Richard Lloyd*** (1860-98), who died at sea in December 1898.

Josiah Lloyd* (1822-66), Long Street, was master of the *Doctor Bunting* 1855-61, the *Sea Queen* 1862-64, and of the *Isabella Saunders* 1864-66 sailing to the Americas when he was drowned on 29 September 1866. By his wife, Esther, he had a son, **Josiah Lloyd**, born in 1850, mate on the *Forest Prince* 1878-79, the *Muriel* 1882-86, and the *Lucia* in 1887.

Stephen Lloyd (1743-1800), ordained minister at Brynberian Independent Chapel in 1770, was the owner of the sloop *Mayflower* which he left in his will to his daughter, Mary, the wife of **Benjamin Davies** (1762-1849).

Thomas Lloyd of Cwmgloyn, a gentleman farmer, a magistrate and sheriff of the county of Pembroke in 1771, built three ships of oak grown on his own estate that were engaged in the coastal trade, one of which, *Yr Hebog* (The Hawk), was the subject of a poem (pp. 23, 105). He died unmarried, the last of the Lloyds of Cwmgloyn, on 21 January 1788.

Thomas Lloyd, Dandre, went to sea in 1788 and was a mariner for 47 years.

Thomas Lloyd (1843-76) was master of the barque *Evening Star* that was wrecked on Little Cavan Island, Cayman, on 18 October 1876. The master and ten of the crew, including **David Morris** (1842-76) from Newport, were lost while the survivors were landed at Montego Bay.

William Lloyd, Bettws and, later, of Penfeidr, shipwright (p. 21), was one of 'the elders of the Independent meeting house', otherwise Ebenezer Independent Chapel, and was 'for many years one of the main pillars of the cause at Newport.' He gave land in Lower St Mary Street upon which the present chapel was built and in his will, dated 27 May 1833, he left the sum of £400 in trust towards the ministry at the chapel but, on account of some flaw in the will, the money could not be transferred. He died at Penfeidr in 1834 leaving his shares in the brig *Artuose* and in the schooner *Charlotte* to his relatives.

Henry Longhurst (1812-61), master of the *Cherub*, was drowned at sea on 24 December 1861.

John Luke* (1870-1954), master of the *Holmlea* 1898-1909 was the son of Owen Luke, Penbrynkys. After he retired from the sea he lived at Mount View.

John Marsden, born in 1859, master mariner, lived at Belle Vue, Penybont. He served as mate on the *Hartburn* in 1887-88 and had three sons who were seafarers: **John G. Marsden**, born in 1893, **Llewelyn Marsden**, born in 1895 and **Edward C. Marsden**, born in 1905, who was master of the *Uria* that was torpedoed and sunk in January 1941, and of the *Benedick* in 1947.

Samuel Marsters, born in 1820, was master of the *Wild Horse* 1857-59, the *Wilmington* 1862-63, the *Regina* 1864-66 sailing to Quebec, the *Ella Moore* 1868-70, and the *Sultan* 1882-84.

Daniel Mathias (1841-1909), Lower St Mary Street, mariner, by his wife, Margaret, had a son, **William Mathias** (1867-86).

David Mathias, mariner, born in 1836, was the son of William Mathias (1788-1861) of Nevern, lime burner and landlord of the Crown and Anchor Inn, Parrog, by his wife, Sarah. In his will, William Mathias bequeathed 'the Crown and Anchor, and the lime kiln attached thereto' to his son, David Mathias, with a condition that his daughters, Anne, Mary, Martha and Corbetta, should have the right to make it their home until they were married. His brig, the *Diligence*, was to be shared between his wife, daughters and sons, David and John Mathias.

David Mathias (1839-1918), son of Mary Mathias, West Street, and later of St Mary Street in 1871, was master of the *Ondara* 1867-70, and of the *New Wabena* 1870-73, the *Abana* 1874-80 and the *Andola* 1886. He married Margaret, daughter of **Thomas Will**iams Ondara House, and had two sons, William and Samuel, and three daughters, Emily Wabena, who married Albert Herbert James, bank manager; Anne Marie, who married Dr George Henderson Baird of Dublin, and Margaret Jane who married John Russell Peel of Tiverton. He was mayor 1906-08. He died at Ondara House on 21 October 1918.

Henry Mathias (1808-80) was master of the *Thomas & Frances* 1856-65.

John Mathias was master of the sloop *Swift* 39 tons that was built at Newport in 1825 and was lost in 1837.

John Mathias was master of the *Sabrina* in 1854 and was pensioned in 1855.

Samuel Hughes Mathias* (1869-1951) was the son of David Mathias, mate, and his wife, Margaret (née Young), of Woodville Terrace, Lower St Mary Street. He was master of the *Italiana* 1902-04, *Heathbank* 1904, *Runo* 1906, *Amin* 1906, *Bala* 1912-13, *Dunraven* 1913-17, *Euston* 1917, *Radcliffe* 1917, *Llangorse* 1918, *Asgard* 1919-20, *Alma* 1920-21, *Boverton* 1921-24, *Flinston* 1925-28 and *Llanfair* 1928-30. A letter from the High Commissioner for Newfoundland, dated 30 September 1925, thanked him and his crew for rescuing the crew of the Newfoundland vessel *G. D. Bailey* in the Atlantic on 4 November 1924. Captain Sam, as he was known, married Jane Sarah, daughter of **John Richards** (1845-1906), Hill Park, and it was said that he had been given the adjoining house, Hilston, by his father-in-law as a wedding present. He died on 10 February 1951.

Thomas Mathias* 1837-65, Bettws, was master of the barque *Lily* of Scarborough that was lost with all hands in the Cattegat bound from Kronstadt to Leith on 1 June 1865.

Thomas Gilbert Mathias,* master mariner, son of Daniel Mathias, Glan-nant, Goat Street, by his wife, Mary Ellen (née Gilbert), went to sea with **David Harris**, Oakfield, and was on the *King Lud* when it was sunk by the German cruiser *Emden* in the Indian Ocean in 1914 (p. 56). He later served on the *City of*

Singapore and the *City of Durham* He married Florence Kato, daughter of **David John Evans** (1864-1900), master mariner, and their son, **David Mathias**, served on the Cross-Channel Service between Fishguard and Rosslare.

William Mathias (1780-1812) was master of the *Mary Anne* in 1882.

William Mathias (1867-86), son of **Daniel Mathias**, mariner, died at Bahia, Brazil, on 28 July 1886, aged 19 years.

Frederick John Meyrick (1914-47), second mate on the *Lepton*, died on board following an accident at Pladjoe, Sumatra, on 23 October 1947.

John Meyrick* (1816-1902), was the first master of the topsail schooner *Alice Williams* 137 tons that was built at Llanelli and named after the owner's wife, who was suitably portrayed in a handsome figurehead, and launched on 3 January 1855. The vessel was taken on her maiden voyage to Falmouth by Capt. Meyrick with a mate, two able bodied seamen, and two apprentices. She sailed mostly to the Mediterranean and the Baltic ports. In February 1928, in a gale off St Ann's Head, she was abandoned by the crew and ran on to the rocks at Skokholm where she was found by the author and naturalist R. M. Lockley who had recently occupied the island and was in the process of renovating the house and out-buildings, where he established the first bird observatory in Britain. He purchased the wreck with its cargo of 200 tons of coal for £5. The ship's timbers were used to refurbish the buildings and her wheel is fixed to the chimney breast in the refectory, a converted barn known as the Wheelhouse. The white-faced figurehead, with piercing blue eyes and roses in her hair, stood for some years above the landing place to welcome visitors to the island, but it has now had to be taken indoors. John Meyrick was master of the *Rhoda* 1868-72. By 1881 he was living at St Mawes, Cornwall, his wife, Sarah, being from there. He later moved to 2 Mount Pleasant Terrace. He was mayor of Newport 1901-02 and died during the latter year.

John Meyrick, born in 1870, was master of the *Anapa* 1911-12, *Almeriana* 1913-14, *Cundall* 1917-19, *Lexington* 1922-3, and of the *Bay State* in 1925.

James Cledwyn Luke Michael (1900-35), master mariner, son of Carbetta Michael (née Luke), Ocean House, and nephew of **John Luke**, master mariner, died at Brooklyn, New York, on 7 April 1935.

David Morgan (1823-63) was mate on the *Thomas Bayne* that sailed in 1863 from Llanelli to New York and was lost with all hands.

David Morgan of Milford married his cousin, Eleanor, daughter of John John of Alltclydach. He raised money on the house, Alltclydach, to purchase a vessel which sank without security and he lost all his money. He was then taken as a mate on his ship by his cousin, **Morris John**, but on the way home from Oporto he died, leaving a wife and a young family.

David Morgan was master of the 31 ton smack *Pride of Wales* at Newport in 1880.

James Morgan (1847-76), mate on the *Allum Ghur*, died at Port Louis on 16 March 1876.

James Stephen Morgan, Danyllan, Upper St Mary Street, was a steward.

John Morgan* (1803-25), mariner, son of the Rev. John Morgan by his wife, Mary, was drowned off St Petersburg on 10 July 1825.

John Morgan, born in 1828, was mate on the *British America* 1865 sailing to Quebec, the *Walsgrif* 1865-66 and the *Slains Castle* in 1873.

Morris John Morgan* (1905-80), Talar Wen, Dandre, master of the *East Wales* and of the *West Wales* and Swansea pilot, was the son of David Morgan, Spring Hill Terrace. He married Vera, daughter of Tom Evans, draper, Manchester House. He was mayor in 1972-74 and he gave a new oak pulpit to Bethlehem Baptist Chapel in memory of his parents.

Owen Morgan (1807-72), master of the *Valiant* 1856-66 and of the *Ellen* 1868-67 had a son, **Thomas Morgan**, who lost his life at sea in 1864, aged 20 years.

Thomas Morgan, master of the smack *Joan & Elizabeth* 21 tons at Newport in 1878 and of the 26 ton smack *Thomas* in 1882.

William Morgan, born in 1840, was mate on the *British Tar* that was wrecked in 1862, and on the *Assayr* 1865-66.

John Morgans, born in 1845, was master of the *Beech* and was found guilty of default when his vessel was stranded on the Dora Rocks, Cattegat, on 20 October 1879.

David Morris (1842-76), mate on the *Evening Star*, **Thomas**

Lloyd (1843-76) master, was drowned when the ship was wrecked off Little Cavan Island on 18 October 1876.

David John Morris, born in 1869, was master of the *Yarra* 1919-22 and of the *Colac* in 1929 trading mostly along the coasts of Australia.

David John Morris, born in 1896, was master of the *Clan Macnab* 1925-7 and of the *Clan MacInnes* 1930-34 and became marine superintendant of the Clan Line, Glasgow.

John Morris, master of the *Christian* at Newport in 1876.

John Morris, master of the 22 ton smack *Mary Ann* at Newport in 1882.

John Morris* (1815-38), son of **Thomas Morris** (1787-1819), was master of the schooner *Jane* of Newport that was lost with all hands in a gale on voyage between London and Galway in August 1838.

John Morris (1822-1903), who built Ivy House, was master of the *Jane Morrison* of Cardiff, probably a troop transport at the Crimean War, that was lost at Balaklava on 14 March 1856. He was master of the *Xiphias*, a 534 ton barque, 145 ft long, 30 ft wide and 18 ft deep, sailing to Miramichi, Philadelphia, and Bahia, until 1862 when the vessel was wrecked off San Francisco, and of the *Forest Queen* 1867-81 sailing to the Americas. By his wife, Margaret, he had two seafaring sons and two daughters who married master mariners: **Thomas Richard Morris** (1866-1918. **John Ernest Morris**, born in 1869. Margaret Frances, who was active as a Sunday School teacher at Ebenezer Chapel and promoter of temperance, married **David Jones**, Tycornel, and Mary Anne, married **John Williams** (1810-58).

John Ernest Morris, born in 1869, master mariner, died unmarried. He was a member of the Pint Club, a small select group that met each evening in the back room of the Golden Lion, where he used to regale the members with tales of his travels. He sat on a low chair on the left side of the fireplace, puffing away at his pipe and making frequent use of the cuspidor that had been placed conspicuously at his feet so as to prevent him spitting into the fire. When he was told that an atomic bomb had flattened Nagasaki, his response was: 'Bloody nonsense. I know Nagasaki well – a big city with great big houses and buildings. Matter of fact, I knew a girl in

Nagasaki, Natasha was her name. No, they'd never flatten a big city like that.' Each year he brought a basinful of strawberries for Betty, the daughter of the Golden Lion. 'How do you manage to grow such fine strawberries,' he was asked, 'I don't weed 'em,' he replied. 'You see, if I don't weed 'em, the birds in the trees won't see them, and the worms on the ground get 'tangled in the weeds, and I get the strawberries!'[26]

Joshua Morris (1891-1975), son of Thomas Morris of Cippin Stone by his wife Mary Longhurst, was master of the *Monitora* which was sunk by hostile action on 20 October 1915. He married Mary Gladys Thomas, daughter of **James Thomas** (1845-1923) of West End.

Richard Morris (1790-1878), Parrog, master mariner, by his wife, Mary (1776-1859), had two sons: **David Morris** (1815-38), mariner, and **Thomas Morris** (1820-65).

Robert Morris, master of the brig *Royal Recovery* 82 tons built in 1805 at Kidwelly but registered as of 'Newport, Cardigan'.

Thomas Morris* (1787-1819), master of the sloop *William & Anne* 88 tons built at Newport in 1790, died on 9 January 1819. By his wife, Jane, he had a son, **John Morris** (1815-38).

Thomas Morris* (1820-65), master of the *Janet Wilson* in which he sailed to North America until 1858 when the vessel foundered, and of the *Harmony*, with **Thomas Rowlands** and **William Thomas** (1847-65) on board, that was lost with all hands off the coast of Scotland on her homeward passage from Quebec on 29 December 1865.

Thomas Morris (1835-85), Castle Street, mariner, died of bronchitis at Gijon in Spain, on 4 November 1885.

Thomas Morris, seaman, lost his life during the 1914-18 war.

Thomas Richard Morris (1866-1918), son of **John Morris**, Ivy House, was master of the *Cliftonian* that was sunk by torpedo on 6 December 1917. He died at sea on 13 November 1918 while serving on the *Atlantic City*. He was married to Anne, daughter of **David Owen**, master mariner, Grove Park.

William Morris (1912-43) lost his life at sea on 27 March 1943 while serving as quarter-master on the *City of Guildford*.

William (Willie) Morris, marine engineer on oil ships trading with Aruba. His father, John Morris, kept the *Newport Boarding*

Book giving particulars of all the ships landing at Newport between 1876 and 1900, excerpts from which were published by his brother, Vincent Morris, in *The County Echo* in 1958. The book has been deposited by his nephew, John P. Morris, at the Pembrokeshire Record Office.

R. H. R. Nesbitt, 2 Mount Terrace, master mariner, had a son, **Jack Nesbitt**, born in 1905, who was also a master mariner.

David Nicholas* was master of the sloop *Jane* 28 tons built at Aberporth, that was lost with all hands, including his son, John, 'in the month of November *anno domini* 1798,' as stated on his gravestone, which is the earliest date found on a maritime tombstone in St Mary's churchyard. He was married to Anne Williams (1757-1831) who left in her will, proved on 20 January 1832, five dwelling houses situated in West Street, High Street and St Mary Street, together with freehold lands and shares in the the sloops *Nelson* 42 tons built at Cardigan 1805, *Mary Ann* 23 tons built at Newport 1810, *Lily* 45 tons built at Bideford 1798, the brigs *Victory* 118 tons built at Newport in 1811, *Martha* of Dinas 123 tons built at Appledore 1819, *Diligence* 114 tons built at Newport in 1814, *Eliza* of Dinas 135 tons, foreign-built, the schooners *Speculator* 76 tons built at Aberystwyth 1804 and *Lady Day* of Fishguard 128 tons, 'Capt. David Harries of Dinas ship,' and 'Jacky Griffith of Dinas ship.' By his wife Anne, David Nicholas had two sons who were seafarers: **John Nicholas** who perished with his father on the *Jane* in November 1798, and **Evan Nicholas*** (1797-1877), master of the brig *Victoy*, pensioned on 1 January 1859. His mother, in her will, left him a dwelling house in West Street, 'commonly called Lewis Williams's house' and a house in St Mary Street and shares in the *Victory*, the *Speculator* and the *Nelson*, together with a share of her 'freehold lands called Westfield and Little Field'. He lived in Market Street in 1832, on Parrog in 1835, at East View in 1844, in St Mary Street in 1871 and at Penrallt in 1873. By his wife, Frances (1811-45), daughter of John and Mary Owen, Rhosmaen Farm, Nevern parish, he had two sons and a daughter: **John Owen Nicholas*** (1832-44) who lost his life at sea on board the *Victory* off Cape Clear, Ireland, on 20 June 1844 aged 12 years. **David Nicholas*** (1833-49) who died at sea on board the *Victory* when it sank off the Skelligs Rocks, co. Kerry, aged 15 years, and Frances Mary Ann, who ran the Queen's Hotel for a time, and then the Sloop Inn, Parrog, died unmarried at West End Cottage on 1 February 1903 aged 68 years.

David Nicholas* (1803-77), started his seafaring career sailing in 1820 with his father, **Thomas Nicholas** (1757-1843), Mount Pleasant, master mariner. He bought the vessel *Ocean*, in 1832 which he exchanged in 1852 for the brig *Excel* 213 tons, built at Milford in 1854 by **Levi Havard**, in which he sailed until he retired in 1867. He was a prominent member of Tabernacle Calvinistic Methodist Chapel. He married Anne Jones of Llansawel and had a son and a daughter. The son, Thomas Nicholas (1850-1933) married Martha Jane Evans and had a son, **David Theodore Nicholas**, (1893-1980), marine engineer. Jane, the daughter, married **William Thomas Jermain**.

David Nicholas (1860-1952), son of Morris Nicholas, Nevern, went to sea as a boy in 1877 on the schooner *Mary Eliza* of Cardigan 64 tons. He was master of the *Alderley* 1894-97, the *Aral* 1897-1904, the *Trojan* 1909-17 and the *Penrhydd* 1920-25. He lived at Allt Goch, Nevern, and married Annie, daughter of **John Thomas**, Rhosnanty, at Ebenezer Chapel on 8 January 1884. He died in February 1952

James Nicholas, son of **William Nicholas**, Steeple View, was a master mariner. He lived at Goodwick and was buried at Manorowen.

Joshua Nicholas, St Mary Street, born in 1817, was master of the *Economist* 1868-76, the *Daniel* 1876-77 and the *Baltic* in 1878.

Thomas Nicholas (1757-1843), Mount Pleasant, master mariner, married Jane Davies of Cardigan, sister of **John Davies** (1766-1835), and had a son and three daughters who married master mariners: **David Nicholas*** (1803-77), master of the *Excel,* Phebe Nicholas, married **David Havard** (1801-43), master mariner, Anne Nicholas, married **William Havard** (1803-50), master mariner, and Mary Nicholas married **Rowland Rowlands** (1794-1852), master mariner, who had previously married Anne, daughter of **John Havard** (1771-1839).

Thomas Nicholas, Pendre, master of the *Hope* 182 tons, the largest vessel built at Newport, died on 26 August 1826 aged 39 years.

Thomas Nicholas, born in 1817, was mate on the *Meteor* sailing to Sydney in 1858.

Tom A. Nicholas (1894-1942), son of Daniel and Mary Nicholas, Parrog Road, died on 31 October 1942 while serving as chief officer on the MV *Fook On*. He was buried at the Stanley Military Cemetery, Hong Kong.

William Nicholas,* Steeple View, born *c.*1852, a ship's carpenter, lost his life at sea in November 1881. His son, **James Nicholas**, master mariner, was buried at Manorowen.

David Owen (*c.*1776-1858) was master and owner of the brig *Ant* of Cardiga, built at the Netpool. He married Elizabeth Owen of St Dogmael's in 1811 where he settled.

David Owen, Grove Park, Penybont, master mariner, a native of Ceredigion, was a deacon at Ebenezer Independent Chapel and treasurer of the Carningli Branch of the Ancient Order of Foresters. His daughter, Anne, married **Thomas Richard Morris** (1888-1916).

David Owen, chief steward, was killed in action 1914-18 war.

James Owen (1844-64), son of Joshua Owen of Glanrhyd, mate on the *Advance*, was drowned at sea on 7 October 1864 while sailing from Liverpool to Tarragona.

John Owen* (1800-56), master mariner, son of William Owen, postmaster, died 24 August 1856 and left £1,500 in his will. By his wife, Elizabth, daughter of **Llewellyn Davies**, he had a daughter, Elizabeth Mary, who married **John Owen** (1835-74).

John Owen (1802-42), son of William Owen, carpenter, was an apprentice on the *Valiant*, **Daniel Evans**, master. He later served on the *William & Anne*, **Thomas Morris**, (1787-1819), master, and on the *Jupiter*, **John Williams** (1782-1812), master, on which he sustained an accident during a storm. He then gave up the sea and was ordained minister at Brynberian Independent Chapel in 1834 and moved to Llysyfran the following year.

John Owen,* (1835-74), High Street, son of William Owen, mariner, was master of the *Southern Empire* and lost his life when the ship foundered at sea on 12 December 1874.

John Owen (1843-86) of the Barley Mow, Market Street, was master of the *Montgomery Castle* 1877-81 sailing to the East Indies and of the *Raglan Castle* 1883-85 sailing to the North Pacific.

John Owen (1877-1918) died on 17 March 1918 while serving as cook on the SS *Cressida*. He was the son of Joshua and Esther Owen and the husband of Keturah (née Davies), Tycoch.

John Lewis Owen,* (1837-74), master of the *Flying Cloud* in 1869 and of the *Southern Empire* that was lost at sea on 12 December 1874 when he was drowned.

William Owen* (1797-1846), master of the schooner *Mary Ellen*, died in Quebec on 5 August 1846.

John Owens* (1880-1947), a native of Cardigan, was master of the *Llandrindod* that was sunk by enemy action and he was held prisoner at Brandenburg, and of the *Radcliffe* 1920-27. He married Elizabeth Hannah, daughter of **Thomas Edwards**, West View, master mariner, and lived at 1 Mount Terrace until he and his wife moved to West View.

Evan Parry, master of the 28 ton smack *Margaret & Ann* at Newport in 1878.

John Peregrine (1842-76), mate on the *Annie Gray*, died at Saigon on 26 January 1876.

David Phillips (1831-59), mate on the *Veloz*, sailed from Liverpool to Bombay on 6 May 1859 and died at sea on 8 October that year.

David Phillips (1856-1817) died at sea through enemy action on 17 April 1917.

James Phillips* (1851-1919), Abertawe House, was master of the SS *Abermaed* from 1883 to 1886 and of the SS *Abertawe* from 1886 to 1901. The *Abertawe*, bound for Tunis with a cargo of 1,850 tons of coal, was pierced by her own anchor at Galetta and beached on 16 February 1900 and was floated on 15 March, with the vessel ashore in harbour. A Board of Trade inquiry found no blame on the master and justified him for beaching. The crew included his brother-in-law, **Morris Lewis**, second engineer, and two seamen, Tom amd John Howells, who were Newport men. One seaman was drowned during the incident. The master also had on board his wife, Anne, daughter of Evan Lewis, Blaenmeini, whom he had married in 1899. The crew presented him with a silver tea service on his marriage together with a painting of the *Abertawe*. His son **Howard Cecil Lewis Phillips**, OBE (1900-61), was master of the *Temple Pier* when it was was captured by the French at Algiers on 3 July

1940 (p. 66). He was later master of the *Coultarn* that was sunk by a German submarine in April 1941, of the *Stanmore* carrying 2,000 tons of ammunition to Italy when it was torpedoed on 4 October 1943, of the Shell Oil tanker, *Hygromia*, sailing to Borneo and Singapore, and of the *Empire Fitzroy* until he retired in 1946. He married Daisy, daughter of Capt. Thomas Jones, superintendent of the Furness Withy Line in the USA. He was appointed an Officer of the British Empire on 8 March 1944 for distinguished war service.

John Phillips (1790-1843), master mariner, died on board the brig *Venus* of Milford on 16 December 1839 at Port-Law, Waterford, and is remembered on the gravestone of his wife, Frances, in Ebenezer graveyard.

Thomas Phillips, born in 1818, was mate on the *Cygnet* in 1857.

Jack Price, Seagull Cottage, ferryman crossing the river from Parrog to Traeth Mawr, for which he charged a penny at low water and two pence when the tide was high. His bent figure and appearance of utter dejection reminded one of the legendary Charon who conveyed the souls of the dead in his boat across the river Styx in the nether world This attitude became acute each winter, when he would go to sea. On one such occasion, **George Adams** met him in the street in Cardiff and took him, despite his protest, into a pub and called for 'two large whiskies'. The barmaid took one look at the woebegone Jack, who hadn't touched a drop, of course, and said 'I'm afraid your friend's had enough already!' His wife was the district nurse and she was his opposite in every way imaginable. She had a lively, porcine face and was always bright and cheerful and prone to make shocking utterances, such as: 'You can always tell the paternity of a child by the way it looks during the first hour of its life, and you'd be surprised at the number of familiar faces I have seen in my time!'

James Price, born *c.*1820, was master of the *Donald McKay* and he had with him his son, **James Price**, aged 17 years, as fourth mate, and **Llewelyn James**, boatswain.

John Price (1866-93), ship's carpenter on the *James Wishart*, was drowned between ship and shore at Bordeaux.

John Protheroe, born in 1845, was master of the *Heptarchy* 1878-81 and of the *Carlo* 1882-85 in the Mediterranean trade.

Abel Rees, born in 1847, was mate on the *Ivanhoe* when he was charged at a naval court at Callao on 4 February 1876 with having ill-treated the master, **David Hughes**. He married Mary, daughter of David and Margaret Evans of the Ship and Castle and had issue. He later became a high class grocer in Cardiff.

David Rees, master of the dandy *Heatherbelle* at Newport 1876.

Edward Rees* (1781-1842) was a Lieutenant, Royal Marines.

James Rees, born in 1859, was a mate on the *Elizabeth Mary* and was discharged in Sydney on 8 July 1886.

John Rees (1866-1930) was master of the *Gelfarg* in 1902, the *Johanna* 1906-07 and of the *Maindy Hill* 1924-29.

Llewellyn Rees, born in 1804, was master of the *Ann* on voyage from Liverpool to Greenland in 1866.

Thomas Rees, born in 1844, was master of the *Aline* 1878-79 sailing to Australia.

Vernon Rees (1927-2004), Parrog Stores, was air mechanic on HMS *Illustious*.

Ebenezer Richards, West Street, a Cape Horner, is remembered as an old man sitting in front of the fire in his greasy sailor's hat, a pair of ebony elephants and a ship in a bottle on the mantelpiece to remind him of his voyaging. He mixed his own tobacco which gave its aroma to the house, and the nicotine had stained his patriarchal beard so that the white hairs were yellow and the grey ones green.

Edward William Richards,* marine engineer, a native of Ferndale, married Clara Nore, daughter of Thomas Griffiths, Cnwce Farm, and lived at 1 Mount Terrace. He died on 27 February 1931 leaving a widow, and five seafaring sons and a daughter who married a sailor: **Thomas Jabez Richards**, born in 1893, master of the *Bachaquero* 1940-45, died in Aruba, **Ward Richards**,* master of the *Pacific*, was lost at sea during the 1939-45 war, **Frederick Richards**,* marine engineer, was drowned at sea, **Neville Richards**, marine engineer, and **George Richards**,* who was educated at St David's College, Lampeter, with a view to taking holy orders but found that his calling was the sea. He was drowned in Bordeaux harbour. Leila, the daughter, married **George Griffiths**, marine engineer.

Granville Richards, master mariner, of Seaglen, married Anne Evans of Clover Hill, Dinas. He was at sea from 1929 until 1974 serving as mate on a number of ships, including the *Jersey City*, **James D. Varney** master, the *East Wales*, **B. W. George** master, the

Llanberis, Fort la Trinité, Uskport, Indore, North Cornwall, Thackeray, Caledonian Princess and as chief officer of the *Bruce*. His brother, **Ivor Richards** served as chief petty officer on minesweepers off the coasts of South Africa during the 1939-45 war.

James Richards* (1820-93), master mariner, by his wife, Mary, had two seafaring sons and a daughter who married a mariner: **David Richards** (1851-78), mate on the *Stallinbro* 1877-78, was drowned when the ship was wrecked on 30 March 1878, **James Richards** (1856-73), was lost at sea in January 1873 aged 17 years, and Anne married **William Nicholas**, Steeple View.

James Ernest Richards* (1887-58), Steeple View, master mariner, was involved in coastal trading in China from 1919 to 1930. He was awarded a silver salver for saving the lives of some fishermen during a storm off the China coast. He married Elizabeth, daughter of **William Nicholas**, Steeple View, where he died on 30 March 1958.

John Richards (1801-61) was master of the *Diligence* in 1858.

John Richards* (1845-1906), Upper West Street and later of Hill Park, was master of the *Astracana* 1883-88, the four-masted *Andelana* 2,579 tons 1892-4, the *Lord Ripon* 1895-7; the 1,998 ton full-rigged four-masted barque *Hilston* 1901-02, and of the *Castleton* in 1903. He died on 30 November 1906 at Greenwich Hospital following an accident. By his wife, Mary Anne, daughter of **Thomas Griffiths** (1830-74), he had four seafaring sons and a daughter who married a sailor:

> **Tom Richards*** was drowned off Cape Town on 9 December 1896 aged 19 years.
>
> **William J. Richards*** (1881-1956), Green Cottage, Long Street, master mariner, married Mary Anne, daughter of John Williams, Cross House, draper.
>
> **John Richards*** (1883-1907), Hill Park, died on 23 November 1907.
>
> **David Richards**, marine engineer, served his apprenticeship at the Cardigan Foundry and was chief marine engineer in the employ of Messrs Watts, Watts & Co., London. He married Edith Lewis, sister of **Cecil Lewis**, before retiring and taking over the Red Lion at Cardigan, where he died.
>
> Jane Sarah married **Samuel Hughes Mathias** (1869-1951).

John Richards* (1846-88), master mariner, sailed on the *Crusader* 1876-83 to Australia. He died at Point-de-Galles, Ceylon, in April 1888. By his wife, Eleanor, he had two sons, **David Gilbert Richards** lost his life at sea in January 1894, and **John George Bowen Richards** (1878-1920), master mariner, settled in New Zealand but died in London.

William Richards, born in 1843, was mate on the *Waverley* in 1888.

William Richards (1846-95), Penrhiw Fach, master mariner, died on 21 March 1895.

William Richards, master mariner, married Frances, daughter of the Rev. John Davies, Gideon, and granddaughter of **Llewhelin Griffiths**.

James Roach, born in 1818, was mate on the *Persia* in 1857.

Thomas Roach,* son of Benjamin Roach of the Mariners Arrms, was master and owner of the sloop-rigged flat *Price Jones* 23 tons built at Flint in 1859, which he had purchased from **David Jenkins** (1810-71).

David Roberts was master of the *Kate* at Newport in 1879.

Humphrey Roberts was master of the schooner *Jedulous* 67 tons at Newport in 1876.

Edward Rogers* (1782-1866), Commander, Royal Navy, lived at Cross House and died there on 11 July 1866.

Clyde Rowlands (1914-46), master mariner, Cromlech Farm. died in hospital in Dar-es-Salaam on 28 November 1946. He is remembered on a gravestone at Blaenwaun Baptist Baptist Chapel where his parents are buried.

John Rowlands, Dandre, master mariner, was a deacon at Ebenezer Independent Chapel from 1844 to 1849. He died before 1860 and his widow married the minister of Ebenezer, the Rev. Samuel Thomas, during whose ministry the chapel was built on land given by **William Lloyd** at a cost of £794.

John Rowlands* (1822-73), of Glanrhyd, Long Street, was drowned on 18 May 1873 and his son, **John Rowlands*** (1846-74), was lost at sea the following year.

Rowland Rowlands* (1794-1852), West Street, was master and later owner of the snow *Mars* 130 tons built on the Mawddach in 1812, trading mostly between Cardiff or London and Dublin and, in

1845, between Dublin and Ostend. He was drowned at Llanelli on 2 April 1852. He married firstly Anne, daughter of **John Havard** (1805-36), who died in 1819 following the birth of a son, **John Rowlands** (1819-81), who was brought up by his aunt, Mary Davies, at Dandre. In 1856 he was master of the *Empire* at Cardiff, a 630 ton vessel sailing to Quebec, but he left the sea and became a ship broker at Cardiff. His father, in his will dated 17 February 1838, left him his shares in the brig *Minerva*. He married Hannah Jones at Newport, Gwent, and had a daughter, Julia Anne, who married **David Havard** (1845-1919) in 1875. The remainder of Rowland Rowland's estate was left to his son by his second wife, Mary, daughter of **Thomas Nicholas** (1759-1840), by whom he had **Thomas Rowlands*** (1824-65), who married Ann, daughter of **John Davies** (1805-36), Cross House, and was mate on the *Harmony*, **Thomas Morris**, master, and on which **William Thomas**, aged 17 years, also served, which left Quebec on 17 November 1865 for Penarth Roads and sank off the Scottish coast on 29 December 1865.

David Salmon (1846-90), Gamallt, was first mate on the *Volta* which had to be abandoned in mid-Atlantic in a storm as her cargo of superphosphate had absorbed water, but the crew was rescued by the barque *Achilles* of Memel. He was the master of the *Victory* from 1876 to 1884 sailing to the Americas, and of the *Queen of the North* 1883-87. He lived at Swansea where he died on 16 April 1890. A gravestone to his memory was erected in Nevern churchyard by his brother, Llewellyn Salmon, of Pontardawe.

William Salmon (1835-65) was mate on the *Diligence* in 1862 and on the *Estephania* when he was drowned on homeward passage from Newfoundland.

William Salmon, born in 1899 at Brithdir Bach, was master of the *Quebec City* in 1935. He married Marjory, daughter of **William Roach Thomas** and went to live in South Africa.

David Samuel* (1828-80), master mariner, died at Swansea on 25 March 1880, and he and his wife, Lettice (1817-76), are remembered on the gravestone of James Thomas, Feidrgerigog, Newport, in St Mary's churchyard.

Frederick Davies Seaborne, born in 1859, was master of the *Tolosa* in 1899.

Frederick Seaborne* (1789-1851), a native of Fishguard, lived in Seaborne House, West Street, and in 1828 he was master of the brig *Eliza* of Cardigan owned by **Owen Harries**. His son, **Frederick Seaborne*** (1831-88), sailed as mate on several vessels including the *Essex* which sprang a leak while sailing from New York to Queenstown (Cork) and was abandoned in a sinking condition on 5 July 1865, but the crew was taken off by the *Constantia* of Bremen. He was first mate on the barque *Georgiana* of Liverpool in December 1870 sailing from Rio de Janeiro to Mobile with a cargo of coffee but on Mobile Bar the ship was grounded and became a wreck. He was drowned at sea on 14 February 1888. By his wife, Elizabeth, daughter of **John James**, master mariner (1807-1902), he had three seafaring sons:

> **John James Seaborne*** (1870-1956), master mariner, was a quiet, gentle man but fond of a practical joke. He lived at Seaborne House, West Street, opposite James Thomas, Bohemian Stores, who, having retired spent his time standing in the bay window of the former shop watching the world go by. One day a horse stopped in front of the house and deposited what was known in polite circles as a 'mare's nest'. James Thomas immediately went to the garden shed at the back of the house to fetch a bucket and shovel so as to collect the manure for the benefit of his rhubarb. Seaborne, seeing this from his parlour window, nipped across the road and stuck a small Union Jack upon the steaming little pyramid. James Thomas came rushing out with his bucket and was in the act of placing his shovel under the heap when he saw the flag. He simply froze.[27]
>
> **Frederick Owen Seaborne**, DSC* (1871-1930), master of the *City of Baroda* that was sunk by enemy action on 6 June 1917, and of the *Croxteth Hall* that was sunk on 19 November 1917. He was awarded Lloyd's Medal for Meritorious Service on 24 December 1918 for 'gallant conduct on the occasion of the engagement of the *Newby Hall* with an enemy submarine on 13 September 1918' and the Distinguished Service Cross 'in recognition of zeal and devotion to duty shown in carrying on the trade of the country during the

war.' He was master of several ships of the City Line from 1919 to 1930, including the *City of Chester*. He married Bella, daughter of John Mathias, and died at Newport News, USA, on 5 August 1930.

David Bowen Seaborne* (1874-1923), master of the *Horby Grange*.

James Seaborne, born in 1818, was master of the *Sampson* in 1856-58. After his death, his widow Mary Seaborne, kept the Llwyn-gwair Arms. His son, **Frederick Davies Seaborne**, was master of the *Tolosa*.

James Seaborne* (1879-97) lost his life at sea in 1897, aged 18 years.

David Shadrach (*c*.1788-1869), master mariner, was landlord of the Dolphin Inn in West Street in 1841. His son, the Rev. Benjamin Shadrach, rector of Llanllawer and Llanychllwydog, married Mary, widow of **John Thomas** (1804-47), West End.

John Shadrach, born in 1809, was master of the *Hibbert* 1823-23, the *Harvey Galbraith* 1854-56 sailing to Bahia, and was mate on the *Astarte* and on the *Providence* of Liverpool 1855-56. He and his family settled in Liverpool where he died in 1862. His son, **David Shadrach** (1838-77), mate on the barque *Edward Percy* to San Francisco, Valparaiso, Melbourne and Bombay, was found drowned in Sydney harbour on 11 December 1877.

William Shadrach, born in 1794, was master of the *Diligence* of Milford in 1820. In 1861 he kept a school at Newport.

David Rees Stephens of Hafan, formerly Mauritius, master mariner, was born in 1867, the son of John Stephens, blacksmith, Upper St Mary Street. He left no issue but his brother, Jack Stephens, blacksmith, Craig-y-nos, Parrog Road, had four seafaring sons: **David Stephens**, master mariner, **John Evans Stephens**, born in 1892, master mariner, **Willie Stephens**, master mariner, and **Evan Percy Stephens**, born in 1900, master of the *Aymeric*, the *Larch-bank*, and the *Samuta* between 1939 and 1947.

Benjamin Thomas, (1827-92), West Street, was mate on the *Sophia* that was abandoned at sea on 13 November 1857, on the *City of Lincoln* in 1858, on the *Madawaska* 1859-61 and master of the *Humber* 1878-81 and of the *Asiana* 1883-84.

Benjamin Thomas, master of the 72 ton *Speculator* 1811-19, had to leave the sea as a result of a fall. He married Anne, widow of **Thomas Williams**, Ocean House, and had four daughters, three of whom married master mariners: Mary to **John Thomas** (1804-47), Hannah Jane to **Thomas Griffiths** (1830-74) and Anne to **Thomas Williams** of Ondara House.

Daniel Thomas, born in 1829, sailed as mate on the *Ondara* from Cardiff to Monte Video 1865-66, on the *Madawaska* 1867 to Quebec and on the *Arina* 1887-88.

David Thomas* (1799-1830), West Street, was mate on the schooner *Artuose* 100 tons built at Cardigan in 1823. He was drowned when the vessel sank off the Tusker Rock, near Tiree, on 20 November 1830 and was buried at Kilmichalog.

David Thomas, born in 1813, was master of the *Lord Stanley* of London in 1851, of the *Douglas* of London 1856-61 and of the *Brisbane* 1868-69 sailing to Madras.

David Thomas, born in 1817, was master of the *Princess Alexandra* 1864-67 and mate on the *Thomas Vaughan* in 1871.

David Thomas (1819-87) was master of the *D'Israeli* of Milford 1851-52, of the *Robert Jones* of Caernarfon 1856-58, and of the *Madawaska* 1859-61. He was pensioned in 1867. He lived at the Ship Afloat, now Seagull Cottage, and afterwards at Fern Cottage. His daughter married **John Davies** (1843-1923), and had three sons who were seafarers.

David Thomas (1832-78), Bank Terrace, Long Street, was mate on the *Froas* when he died of yellow fever at Rio de Janeiro on 7 April 1878.

David Thomas, born in 1842, master of the *Flying Cloud*, with **John Davies**, Fountain Cottage as mate, that was lost on 29 December 1868, of the *Planet* and of the *Balnaguith* between 1869 and 1875.

David Thomas, master and owner of the smack *Resolution* at Newport in 1880.

David Thomas of the Angel Temperance Hotel, Long Street, mariner, was the son of Daniel Thomas, Parrog Arms, the story-teller, who used to refer to him as Davy in some of his tales. 'My son Davy came home from Japan, on one occasion,' he stated, 'and he put a small seed in my hand. "Plant that in the garden," he said, and this I did and before a month was out it had grown so big that a man came from the Council saying that the neighbours were complaining that its roots were undermining their houses. It took me days to get the old cabbage down and then we cut it up into pieces and shared it among the people of the town.' A reference to an increase in the local rabbit population, on another occasion, brought from Daniel the expected comment that it was nothing to compare with the plague of rabbits on the Warren that no one was able to control. 'They tried trapping and snaring, and brought ferrets and dogs,' he recollected, 'but of no use. Then Davy came home from the sea and brought with him a sort of net that he had bought in America. It was made of silk, the like of which I had never seen before. "Bring it over to the Warren," I said to him one night, and over we went and spread the net over the rabbit holes. We went over the next morning and found the net full of rabbits, hundreds of them, and I didn't know what to do with them. As it happened, a little Irish schooner, the *Water Lily* had just finished unloading on the Parrog and I sold them to the captain who loaded his ship with them and took them to Ireland.'[28]

David Thomas, boatswain, was lost at sea during the 1939-45 war.

David Glyn Thomas, born in 1894, son of David John Thomas of Pantyrhedyn, was master of the *W. H. Libby* in 1941.

Ernest Thomas, Anchor House, son of Jacob Thomas, Brynhyfryd, was steward on the *Idomeneus*, **David Owen Davies** master.

Henry Thomas* (1836-76), master of the ship *Lyras*, died at Rio de Janeiro on 19 March 1876.

Herman J. Thomas (1897-1941), son of Frederick John Thomas by his wife Margaret, was chief engineer on the SS *Tregarthen* of London when the vessel was torpedoed on 6 June 1941 and he lost his life.

James Thomas, born in 1827 in Milford, sailed as master of the *Talbot* 1863-69 to Bombay, Shanghai, Melbourne, Auckland and Cape Town. In 1881 he lived at the Plough Inn.

John Thomas (1804-47), West End, was master of the snow *Venus* of Milford 97 tons built at Carmarthen in 1808 sailing to London, Cork and Greenock until it foundered at sea in 1847 with the loss of all hands. He had married, on 2 May 1844 at St Mary's Church, the Rev. Benjamin Shadrach, rector of Llanllawer and

Llanychllwydog officiating, Mary, daughter of **Benjamin Thomas**, master mariner, of Parrog, by his wife, Anne, widow of **Thomas Williams**, Ocean House, by whom he had a son, **John Thomas** (1848-84), who was second mate on the *Ondara* when the ship was lost on 19 September 1870 and he was among the survivors. He was master of the *Abana* from 1881 until he died on 28 April 1884 at Calcutta and was buried there in the Lower Circular Road Cemetery. Mary Thomas married, as her second husband, the Rev. Benjamin Shadrach in 1854 and had a daughter, Elizabeth Anne Shadrach who married **James Thomas** (1845-1923), Glanffynnon, Bwlch-mawr, Dinas, master of the *West Australian* 1876-79 who died on 1 October 1923 leaving a son, **John Shadrach Thomas** (1894-1969), master mariner, who settled in Australia, and a daughter, Mary Gladys Thomas, who married **Joshua Morris** (1891-1975).

John Thomas (1819-98), Rhosnanty, was master of the *James Seed* in 1874 sailing from Quebec to Swansea with copper ore when the ship was run down by the vessel *Norma* on the St Lawrence river. His daughter, Anne, married **David Nicholas** (1860-1952).

John Thomas, born in 1820, was master of the *Cherub* in 1866.

John Thomas* (1825-59), master of the barque *Bessy* of Milford, was unwell when the vessel arrived at Alloa, Firth of Forth, on 9 November 1859 and he died two days later. He was married to Elizabeth, daughter of **David Griffiths** (1800-71).

John Thomas (1828-74), Penybont, son of John Thomas, stone-mason, of New England, Cilgwyn Road, was master of the *British Tar* from 1859 until 1863 when it was wrecked, of the *Anne Wilson* 1863-66 sailing to North America, and of the *Veteran* that was wrecked in Fraserburgh Bay in November 1867 and he was drowned. He had two brothers at sea, **Thomas Thomas** (1825-63) and **Levi Thomas**.

John Thomas (1856-1928), Cemaes House, was mate on the *Jungfrau* 1882-84 and master of the *Aral* 1904-09 and of the *Luz Blanca* which was sunk by a German submarine on 5 August 1918. He was deacon and treasurer at Ebenezer Independent Chapel.

John Thomas, born in 1860, mate on the *Rosella* 1887-88, lost his certificate on the SS *Vauxhall* when it was sunk by enemy action on 25 April 1917, and lost it again on the SS *Alston* which was attacked by a submarine later that year.

John Thomas, master and owner of the 21 ton smack *Punch* at Newport in 1876.

John Thomas, master and owner of the *Jane & Margaret* 24 tons at Newport in 1879.

John Thomas, master of the *Tivyside* at Newport in 1884.

John Thomas, seaman, was lost at sea during the 1914-18 war.

John Thomas, son of Morris Thomas, Llystyn Mill, was master of one of Beynon's vessels of Milford.

John L. Thomas* (1889-1915), assistant engineer, son of the Rev. and Mrs Thomas, Major House, died when the SS *Falaba* was torpedoed on 28 March 1915.

Joshua Thomas* (1822-56), master of the brig *Sampson* of Newport, was married to Mary Anne Francis.

Levi Thomas sailed as mate on the *Veteran* with his brother, **John Thomas** (1828-74), and on the *Caledonian* in 1875.

Llewellyn Thomas, 2 Bank Terrace, was boatswain on the *Temple Pier* when he and his son, **Myrddin Thomas**, were taken prisoner (p. 66).

Morris Thomas, born in 1815, was master of the *Isabella* in 1864 and mate on the *Evoe* in 1866.

Morris Thomas (1835-68) was master of the *Venetia* that was last heard of on 19 January 1868 and he was presumed drowned.

Rees Thomas* (1810-66), master and owner of the schooner *Gleaner* of Cardigan 97 tons, made a voyage to the Baltic in 1859. His widow, Catherine (née Mathias), married **Jacob Beer** in 1873.

Roachie Thomas, marine engineer, son of **William Roach Thomas**, Hill Park, married Violet Isaac, daughter of **William Isaac**, Gwylfa.

Samuel Young Thomas (1832-50), son of David Thomas and his wife, Mary (née Young), was drowned at sea on 1 April 1850 and buried at Kingstown (Dublin).

Thomas Thomas (1825-63), a brother of **John Thomas** (1828-74), Penybont, and **Levi Thomas**, was master of the *India* of South Shields when he died in the Gulf of Lawrence. He was married to Ellen Thomas of High Street, by whom he had a son, **Thomas Davies Thomas**, born in 1855, who was mate on the *Euxine* 1888.

Watkin Thomas (1844-70), was master of the *Ondara* which sailed on 11 June 1870 from Swansea for Tabasco, Mexico, and had to be abandoned at sea on 19 September when he was drowned. Capt. Roach of the barque *M. E. Corning* of Yarmouth, Nova Scotia, was awarded a binocular glass by the Board of Trade for humanity and kindness to the surviving crew that he had rescued.

William Thomas, born in 1805, was mate on the *Equity* 1860 and on the *Thomas* in 1862.

William Thomas, born in 1817, was master of the *Alert* 1857-61.

William Thomas, born in 1819, was mate on the *Caractacus* that was lost with all hands on 23 November 1852.

William Thomas, born in 1842, was mate on the *Berkshire* 1880-86 and on the *Carnarvonshire* 1886-88, and master of the *Portadown* in 1914.

William Thomas* (1847-65), son of David and Jane Thomas, Parrog, and grandson of Margaret George, second wife of **John Havard** (1771-1839), is commemorated on the gravestone of Margaret Havard as having 'lost his life on the ship *Harmony* near the highland of Scotland, December 29th 1865 aged 18 years.' **Thomas Morris** (1834-65) was master of the ship and **Thomas Rowlands** was mate.

William Thomas (1852-74), mariner, was drowned in the East Bute Basin, Cardiff, on 24 September 1874.

William Thomas, owner of the smack *Miss Sarah* 15 tons trading between Milford Haven and Newport which, after discharging its cargo of culm at Newport, sank off St Ann's Head on 25 August 1877 when her master, **Daniel Evans** (1800-77), and crew of two perished.

William Roach Thomas (1863-1947), Hill Park, by his wife, Charlotte, had a daughter, Marjory, who married **William Salmon**, Brithdir Bach, and a son, **Roachie Thomas** who married Violet, daughter of **William Isaac**, Gwylfa.

John Tudor (1862-1917), Glan-y-don, chief steward, lost his life at sea through enemy action on 20 October 1917. His son, **Ingli Tudor** (1895-1925), was marine engineer on the *Derville*, **Thomas Norman Havard**, master, that was reported lost with all hands on 24 December 1925 after leaving St Anthony, Newfoundland, following a terrific gale.

Jesse Varney,* who came from Buckinghamshire as a game-keeper for Edward Shaw Protheroe at Dolwilym, Llanglydwen, used to cycle to Newport to seek the hand of Mary Anne, daughter of **John Davies** (1825-74), master mariner, Penrallt, whom he married at St Mary's Church in December 1883. He was also sexton, verger, gravedigger, gardener and town crier and, by his wife, he had seven sons, six of whom were seafarers:

James Davies Varney of Glan Towy, Church Street, and later of 1 Cambria Terrace, signed on the three-masted square-rigged barque *Inverness* when he was 15 years of age for an eleven month voyage to Chile, and this was followed by a voyage on the barque *Craigisla* to Chile and Peru. His last voyage in a full-rigged ship was on the *Celtic Monarch* that left Swansea on 13 May 1905 with a crew of 32 men for San Francisco. It took three months before they got round Cape Horn and the ship arrived at San Francisco on Christmas Eve having lost seven men and with only the mizzen royal and topsails remaining. When the repair work was almost complete, on 18 April 1906, twelve of the surviving able seamen went ashore for the night. It was the night of the San Francisco earthquake and they all perished. The ship, with a reduced crew, took on a cargo of timber for Australia but, before she reached Sydney, she was demasted. After repair, she took a cargo of coal to Chile where she was loaded with saltpetre. They had such bad weather rounding Cape Horn that water flooded the hold and when they arrived at Hamburg the saltpetre was a solid block. He joined his first steam ship in 1911 and during the 1914-18 war he was injured in the Dardanelles. He was master of the *Afon Towy* for sixteen years, a vessel owned by Messrs Coombes of Llanelli. In 1939 he was seconded to the Royal Naval Reserve and commanded a corvette escorting Atlantic convoys. He was then in charge of the shore establishment HMS *Gosling* until 1947 when he reverted to the Merchant Navy commanding ships of the Bristol Steam Navigation Company. By his wife, Diza (née Daniel), he had **Thomas (Tom) Daniel Varney** (1920-41), assistant steward, on the *Norman Monarch* of Glasgow, who was lost at sea on 20th May 1941, aged 21 years.

George Davies Varney, master mariner, settled at Weston-super Mare.

John (Jack) Davies Varney, born in 1890, was master of the *Jersey City* 1928-32 and of the *Imperial Valley* 1933-4 and lived at Llanarth.

Thomas Edmund Varney* (1893-1917), able seaman on the *Kariba*, died on 21 April 1917, aged 24 years. His son, **Roderick (Roddy) Varney**, served as a steward on the *Temple Pier* (p. 66).

Walter Varney, Lower St Mary Street, was master of the *Wave* that was one of the last vessels to trade at Newport. His son, **Walter Mascord Varney**, was an engineer in the Royal Navy during the 1939-45 war.

Arthur Varney, Pantyrhedd, Feidr Ganol, mariner. He went to Swansea to join a shp on one occasion and, on the train, he unexpectedly met his brother, Walter, going to Swansea for the same purpose. When they arrived in Swansea Docks they were surprised to find that they were both joining the same ship, and even more so when they discovered that the master of that vessel was none other than their brother, Jack.

Charles Vaughan, mariner, Long Street, son of Benjamin Vaughan, Forest Farm, settled in Australia. Two of his brothers were master mariners: **Eaton Vaughan**, Westgate House, who married Patty Evans, daughter of John Evans of the Commercial (Castle) Hotel, and **James Thomas Vaughan**, Tawelfa, West Street, who married Lydia Edwards of Trewreiddig Farm.

John Vaughan* (1836-1908), master mariner, of the Rising Sun. Pleasant View, the eldest son of Thomas Vaughan of Forest Farm, was married at Bethlehem Baptist Chapel on 12 October 1865 to Mary, daughter of **David John** (1824-76), by whom he had **John Llewellyn Vaughan**, born in 1873, master of the *Roby* in 1900, who married Hannah Williams of Rhosmaen and lived at Penrhiw Fach.

John Vaughan, born 1852, was master of the *Nellie* that was stranded off Santa Anna Island, Brazil, in 1882 for which his certificate was suspened for three months. He was master of the *Ensign* 1883-84 and of the *Santon* 1885-87.

Benjamin Volk* (1807-53), master of the 54 ton sloop *Elizabeth* of Milford that was wrecked in 1843. He died on 24 June 1853 leaving by his wife, Mary, a son, **John Volk*** (1837-61), mariner, who died at Bombay on 5 April 1861 aged 24 years.

Thomas Volk* (1808-45), Soar Hill, a brother of **Benjamin Volk**, was a master mariner, and he had three seafaring sons:

> **David Volk**, born on 10 May 1833 and baptised at Nevern, was an apprentice in 1847 at Llanelli. He married Sophia Maria Bevan of Abingdon and moved to Falmouth where he became a channel pilot. He lost his life on 18 January 1874 whilst pilot of the *Minnehaha* of Liverpool outward bound from Falmouth to Dublin when, during a gale, the vessel struck a rock on St Mary's, Isles of Scilly.

> **Thomas Volk**, (1838-77), was master of the *Simon* from 1865 to 1871 sailing to Trincomalee, and of the *Hampton Court* from 1871 to 1876 sailing to the Americas.

> **John Volk** (1840-56), master of the brig *Hope* of Cardigan 129 tons built in 1799, was drowned on a voyage from Llanelli to Limerick on 8 October 1856.

Benjamin Williams, born *c.*1800, was master of the *Sarah Ann* in 1856.

Benjamin Williams, born in 1846, was master of the *Victoria* that sailed from New York on 9 November 1872 and was not heard of again.

Beynon Williams, Carnorfa, was a gun-layer on ammunition ships during the 1939-45 war.

Daniel Williams , born in 1821, was master of the *Hero* 1856-59, the *Sylph* 1863-63, the *M. M. Jones* 1863-67, the *R. H. Jones* 1867-68 and the *James Gaddarn* 1868-69.

David Williams, born *c.*1783, was master of the schooner *Orielton* 114 tons of Milford in 1837.

David Williams* (1807-38), master mariner, was the son of **Thomas Williams**, master mariner, Ocean House, by his wife Anne (1778-1869), who later married **Benjamin Thomas**.

David Williams, born in 1810, was master of the *Seppings* of Bridgwater that was lost at sea sailing to Quebec on 18 December

1852, of the *Ceres* in 1865, the *Marathon* in 1866 sailing to Bathurst, and the *East Lomond* 1868-69 to New York, Monte Video and Savannah.

David Williams (1814-70), master of the *Sarah* 1860-61 and of the *Allen* 1863-65, the *Edith Morgan* 1866-67 and of the *Catherine Hodges* that sank on 2 October 1870 and he was drowned.

David Williams* (1823-89) was master of the *Edward Beck* in 1863, of the *Eliza Smeed*, discharged by wreck at Egmont Bay, Prince Edward Island, in 1882, and of the *Betsey* in 1887.

David Williams, born in 1823, was mate on the schooner *Alice Williams* from 1857 to 1864, **John Meyrick** master, and was master in 1874 (p. 77).

David Williams (1825-68), master of the *Louisa* 1861-64 sailing to Adelaide, and then of the schooner *Albion* that was wrecked on 13 January 1868 and he was drowned.

David Williams (1831-79), who moved to Lower Fishguard, was drowned when he was master of the *Eagle*, lost in 1879.

David Williams (1846-91), son of **Thomas Williams**, Ondara, was master of the *Asiana* 1877-83, of the *Abana* 1885-86 and of the *Neptune* in 1888. He married Margaret, daughter of John Thomas, Penybanc, and was landlord of the Queen's Hotel, Parrog, at his death in 1891.

David Williams (1850-78), mate on the *Ilione*, was washed overboard off the Cape of Good Hope and drowned on 11 May 1878.

David George Williams* (1863-84), son of **William Williams**, Westfa, was mate on the *Andora* when he died at sea on 28 December 1884.

David George Williams (1894-1963), son of Benjamin Williams of the Llwyngwair Arms, and grandson of **William Williams**, Westfa, was master of the *Victolite* 1931-33, and afterwards superintendent, Imperial Oil. He married Addie, daughter of William Howells (1821-89), master mariner, Roseneath, Dinas, and died on 15 December 1963.

Evan Williams was master and owner of the *Elizabeth* at Newport in 1878.

Henry Williams, *c*.1816, was master of the schooner *Orielton* 114 tons of Milford in 1843.

Ivor Llewellyn Williams, Sunnymead, Parrog, appears as a Mercantile Marine Officer in the 1915 electoral list (p. 118).

James Williams, mariner, served at sea with **William Isaac** (1880-1949). By his wife, Jane, he had eight sons, four of whom were seafarers:

> **Owen Williams**, master mariner, was drowned at Leghorn.
>
> **Freddie Williams** (1902-72) was master of the *Antigone* in 1940 and then of the *Antiope* that was torpedoed in 1942. He was given command of the new ship *Empire Noble*, later renamed *Amicus*, trading along the Australian coast for sixteen years, when it was sold to the Japanese. He then joined the Idwal Williams Line as master of the *Glenavon*, the *Craigwen* and of the *Craigfelen*.
>
> **Bertie Williams** (1911-64) served on various tramp steamers throughout the 1939-45 war.
>
> **Keri Williams** joined the Merchant Navy during the early days of the war serving with his brother, Freddie Williams, and remained with him as third mate until 1953.

John Williams* (1782-1812), master of the *Jupiter*, died on 15 January 1812, leaving a son, **John Owen Williams**, mariner, who sustained an accident on board ship.

John Williams* (1810-58), Long Street, son of David Williams, mariner, of Stone Hill, was master of the schooner *Rival* 103 tons built at Newport, Gwent, from 1855 to 1856. He married Mary Anne, daughter of **John Morris**, Ivy House, and died on 13 June 1858.

John Williams (1839-94) was master of the *Paragon* until the vessel was abandoned at sea in 1880, and then of the *Lady Cartier* 1880-82 and the *Canute* on which he died on 25 April 1894.

John Williams, born in 1849, was mate on the *Montague* that was wrecked in 1883 near Cape Verde, and on the *Betsey* from 1885 to 1888.

John Williams, born in 1858, was mate on the *Mary Thomas* that was stranded on the Munsciar Reef, Malta, on 5 May 1890.

John Davies Williams (1876-1921) was master of the *Tuskar* 1906-10 and of the *Pencarn* in 1920.

Joseph Williams was master of the 23 ton smack *Ann* at Newport in 1876 and of the *Adeona* 19 tons in 1880.

Llewellyn Williams, born in 1808, was master of the *Little Fred* in 1856-57 and mate on the *Thetis* in 1858.

Llewellyn Williams, born in 1813, was master of the *Appleton* that was lost in 1857, mate on the *Thomas Boyne* in 1860-61 and master of the *Elizabeth* from 1862 to 1870.

Thomas Williams (*c.*1770-1809), master mariner, built Ocean House in 1800. By his wife Anne (1778-1869), who later married **Benjamin Thomas**, he had a son, **David Williams*** (1807-38), master mariner.

Thomas Williams, born in 1804, was master of the *Sydney* 1862-63, of the *Llandaff* 1866-69 and of the *Munton* in 1873.

Thomas Williams* (1812-69), of Parrog, was master of the *Sophia* that was lost on 13 November 1857, of the *Ondara* 298 tons a three-masted barque in which he held twenty shares, from 1858 to 1863 and again from 1865 to 1866, with voyages to Monte Video and Quebec. He was master of the *Madawaska* from 1867 until it was lost in 1868. He married Anne, daughter of **Benjamin Thomas** by his wife Anne (1778-1869) and had two sons and a daughter who married a master mariner:

> **David Williams** (1846-91), of the Queen's Hotel.

> **Thomas Watkin Williams** (1852-83), master of the *Shah Jehan* when he died at Mauritius on 20 December 1883, leaving a wife, Anne, aged 40 years, who lived in 1881 with her sister, Sarah Thomas, innkeeper at the Rose and Crown, now Cilhendre, Upper St Mary Street, together with her four children, three of whom had been born in India.

> Margaret, the daughter, married **David Mathias** (1839-1918).

Thomas Williams, born in 1816, was mate, and then master, of the *Meliora* 1859-63 sailing to Buenos Ayres, Hong Kong, Monte Video and Venice.

Thomas Williams, mariner, was one of the deacons of Bethlehem Baptist Chapel who, in 1789, signed with Essex Bowen of Llwyngwair, a conveyance of land on Major Bank upon which the chapel was erected at a rental of five shillings per annum. The timber for building the chapel was brought from Quebec to Cardigan and then along the coast to Newport.

Thomas Williams (1830-90) was shipwrecked while serving as first mate on the *Como* on 7 March 1871 and he died at Oslo in 1890.

Thomas Williams, born in 1836, was mate on the *Cornishman* 1880-81, on the *Armathwaite* in 1888 and on the *Fortescue* in 1895.

Watkin Williams* (1840-80), master mariner, son of William Williams, West Street, mariner, died at sea on 20 February 1880.

William Williams (1812-60), mate on the *Anne Wilson* sailing from Cardiff for Brazil, died at sea on 11 February 1860.

William Williams* (1813-64), master of the *Rhoda* 1855-57, the *Nivisiquit* 1857-61, and of the *Madawaska* 1863-64 sailing to Brazil, died at Cape Verde on 27 January 1864.

William Williams (1833-67) was mate on the *Xiphias* in 1856, the *Victoria* 1857, the *Excel* 1858-59, the *D'Israeli* 1859-60 and on the *Symmetry* 1860-61, and master of the *Lord Riversdale* 1863, the *Wilson* 1864-65, the *George Reynolds* 1865-67 and of the *Cecrops* that sailed from London to New York but was not heard of after 28 November 1867 and he was presumed drowned.

William Williams* (1836-1929), Westfa, Lower St Mary Street, was mate on the *Agamemnon* 1867-72 and master of the *Westfa* from 1879 to 1886 sailing to the South Pacific. He died on 19 August 1929. By his wife, Esther, he had two sons, **David George Williams*** (1863-84), and **William Owen Williams*** (1869-1930).

William Williams, master of the *Lizzie Anne* 24 tons at Newport in 1878.

William Owen Williams* (1869-1930), Westfa, son of **William Williams*** (1836-1929), was master of the *Penolver* from 1915 to 1921. He married Alice Hughes, daughter of **John Hughes** (1846-94) and organist at St Mary's Church.

David Wood (1852-93), Tyrhedyn, was master of the *Clara* 1883-85 and of the *Lucia* 1886-87. He died on 14 June 1893 while serving on the *Ergina*.

John Wood, Goat Street, born in 1825, was master of the *Anne* 1860-62 and 1869-74 and of the *Mary Anne* from 1886 to 1887. By his wife, Elizabeth, he had a son **John Wood** (1872-83) who was drowned on homeward passage in April 1883.

Lewis Wood (1843-90), Tyrhedyn and then of Penybont, was master of the *David Jenkins* 1874-79. the *Emily* in 1881 which foundered, and of the *Hannah* 1882-85. He died in Mauritius on

28 September 1890 while serving on the *Nuako*. He is remembered on his wife's gravestone at Ebenezer together with their son, **David Wood** (1860-78), who died at New Brunswick on 3 November 1878.

Henry James Wylde (1886-1960), mariner, of Woodfield, Church Street, had a ferry boat taking people across the river from Parrog to Traeth Mawr which, after his death, was carried on by his daughter, Daisy. He had two sons who were seafarers: **Thomas James Wylde** (1908-33), mariner, and **John Henry Wylde** (1910-42), boatswain, who lost his life at sea during the 1939-45 war.

David Young, born in 1821, was mate on the *Windermere* from 1861 to 1867.

James Young, born in 1824, was master of the *Falmouth* 1861-62 and of the *Jane Frances* in 1868.

Samuel Young (1832-50) was drowned at sea off the Irish coast on 1 April 1850 and buried at Kingstown (Dublin).

Yr Hebog

(The Hawk)

The launching of a ship at Newport was the subject of a poem written in the latter part of the eighteenth century.[29] The poet, Ioan Siencyn (1716-96), was the son of a cobbler-poet of Llechryd and he followed his father in both those crafts until 1754 when he was persuaded by Griffith Jones, Llanddowror, the founder of the Welsh Circulating Schools, to open a Welsh school at Nevern. Little is known about him apart from the few particulars gathered from his poems. He married Catherine Owen of Aberdyfi by whom he had a son and a daughter but, when he took to strong drink she left him and returned to Aberdyfi. In 1782 he complained woefully of his poverty stricken circumstances and of his suffering from gout to the extent that he had been confined to his bed in his lowly cottage for the past three months. His poems were largely elegies written on the death of local worthies, or begging poems – seeking a pair of large boots to fit his swollen feet, or a cast-off periwig to cover his bald pate. He also wrote in praise to his patron, Thomas Lloyd (1733-88) of Cwmgloyn in the pariah of Nevern.

Thomas Lloyd traced to Gwynfardd Dyfed, the pre-Norman lord of Cemais and, as he died a bachelor, he was the last of his line. He was a progressive farmer, an improving landlord, a Justice of the Peace and Sheriff of the county of Pembroke in 1771 He maintained the traditional custom of hospitality and people came to his house 'as bees come to the flowers' for the benefit of his advice and words of comfort. For a period of six years he provided Ioan Siencyn with accommodation at Cwmgloyn and during that time Siemcyn taught the poor of the parish to read, books for which purpose were provided by the squire, who also provided books for children to read.

Among his other activities Thomas Lloyd built ships that were engaged in the coastal trade. The building of the schooner *Greyhound*, 70 tons, for Thomas Lloyd and Captain Tucker of Sealyham

ham, took place at Aberystwyth, to which Ioan Siencyn wrote a poem to be sung to a popular tune of the time. He entreats the vessel which was under the command of George Lloyd, the Squire's nephew, to return with her hold full of merchandise and to bring gold and silver from the great cities of the world to the delight of the people of Newport.

In another poem Ioan Siencyn celebrates the launching of a 50 ton schooner that had been built at Newport, of oak grown in Thomas Lloyd's own woods in Cwmhebog (hawk valley) and on that account, named *Hebog*.[28] The poet wishes the ship good fortune under her master, John Prichard, as she faces 'the foaming, billowing sea' and calls on Neptune and Triton to protect her as she conveys Squire Lloyd on his visits to his gentry friends in Ireland and in England, and especially, those in north Wales where he would feast at laden dining tables and be entertained by the local bards in the customary manner with the ancient metrical measures of the *cywydd* and the *englyn* and the odes of Taliesin, court poet to the sixth century Urien, king of Rheged, around the Solway Firth, while quaffing the golden barley beer.

Thomas Lloyd later suffered great misfortune and Ioan Siencyn sent him a poem one New Year's Day offering him solace in his distress at the loss of two nephews, Captain William Morgan of the Marines and Captain George Lloyd, and of the *Greyhound*, that had been 'engulfed by the sea' and of *Hebog* that had been sunk by the cruel French.

The literary critic Saunders Lewis used this poem in one of his radio talks to illustrate the nature and continuity of the Welsh literary tradition. He maintained that the whole body of Welsh poetry, along the long line that began with Taliesin, had contributed directly to 'this obscure piece of work by a little known poet in west Wales; it means that you cannot pluck a flower of song off a headland in Dyfed in the late eighteenth century without stirring a great Northern star of the sixth century.'[30]

CÂN *(A Song)*

i ddymuno Llwyddiant i Long Newydd yr Yswain Llwyd o Gwmgloyn a elwir *Hebog*
(to wish good fortune to a new ship built for Squire Lloyd of Cwmgloyn that is called Hebog)

O'r derw cadeiiog, praff goed Cwm-yr-Hebog,
Fe'th wnaed yn Llong fywiog, alluog mewn lli
Yr Hebog mi'th alwaf, yn llong mi'th gyf'rwyddaf,
Boed iti ddianaf ddaioni.

> *From stately oaks, sturdy trees of Cwm Hebog,*
> *Were you fashioned a lively ship, mighty on the flood.*
> *The Hebog I'll call you, as a vessel I'll greet you,*
> *May a harmless good fortune be yours.*

Rhwydd hynt i ti'r *Hebog* o Drefdraeth flodeuog
I'r cefnfor ewynog, cyforog ei faint;
Taen dithau'th adenydd, anghofia'r glas goedydd,
Dysg fyw rhwng lleferydd llifeiriant.

> *God speed you Hebog, from blossoming Trefdraeth*
> *To the foaming deep, abounding in its might.*
> *Spread out your sails, forget the greenwood,*
> *Learn to live in the sound of the sea.*

Daw Neptune a Thriton dros wyneb yr eigion
I'th ddwyn rhag peryglon yn burion dy bryd
A'r cribog fynyddau, haul, lloer a sêr golau,
Fydd i ti'n eu graddau'n gyf'rwyddyd.

> *Both Neptune and Triton will come over the ocean*
> *To save you from danger in your perfect form.*
> *The crested mountains, the sun, the moon, the glittering stars,*
> *In their courses will guide you.*

Dos dithau'n gyweithas, mewn awyr gauadlas,
Myn gadw dy gwmpas fel dewrwas mewn dŵr;
A'th esgyll yn chwarae cyfuwch a'r cymylau,
A'th fronnau'n gwneud holltau'n yr halltddwr.

Go in comity under a blue domed sky,
Keep to your compass, bold servant of the sea,
Your wings flying as high as the clouds,
Your breasts cleaving the salty foam.

Pan ddygn ddamweinio i'r eigion ymrwygo,
A'r tonnau dan ruo am friwio dy fron,
Dy drwyn a'u trywano, dy dorr a'u braenaro,
Dy lyw a'u gwasgaro'n ysgyrion.

When by grievous chance the sea rips
And the waves rage eager to wound your breast,
Your nose will pierce them, your belly will farrow them
Your rudder will scatter as spray.

Ehed dan dy lwythi, ar hyd cefn y weilgi,
Mor gyflym a'r milgi manylgais ar dir;
A dwg dy negesau yn ddidranc tuag adre,
O'r mannau dan hwyliau dy helir.

Speed on, bearing your cargoes over the crests of the waves,
As fleet as the eager greyhound runs on land,
And bear your errands home without mishap
From the places they send you under sail.

Mae arnat ti'r *Hebog* rai morwyr calonnog;
John Prichard yw'th enwog benswyddog yn syth;
Fe'th geidw mewn tymher ar wyneb y dyfnder,
A'i hyder ar fwynder y fendith.

Among your crew, Hebog, there are some cheerful mariners,
John Prichard your well known master a champion fellow.
He will maintain you in good temper on the face of the ocean
With his faith in the gentleness of the blessing.

Bydd di yn was'naethgar i'r Yswain Llwyd hawddgar
O Gwmgloyn yn glaear heb drydar na dig.
Efe a dy biau, a gostodd dy gistau,
Gwna dithau'i eirchiadau'n barchedig.

Be a trusty servant to the generous Squire Lloyd
Of Cwmgloyn, quietly and without chatter or anger;
He owns thee, has paid for thy coffers.
Do thou his bidding reverently.

Fe ddaw wrth eu bleser i'th fwrdd mewn addfwynder,
I rodio'n ddibryder uwch dyfnder y dŵr;
Gael gwel'd terfysgiadau y mor a'i dymherau,
Rheolau cu radau'n Creawdwr.

        He will come gently on board at his pleasure,
        And stride fearlessly above the deep ocean;,
        To witness the turmoil of the sea and its humours,
        As ordained by the grace of our Creator.

Os dygi'n Ysgweier I'r Werddon neu Loegr,
Na tharia di lawer, myn lywio'n dy ol;
Nid cymaint mae'n hoffi cymdeithas y rheiny,
Y Cymry mae'n garu'n rhagorol.

        Should you take the Squire to Ireland or England,
        Do not bide too long before turning homeward,
        He is not so fond of their society;
        The Welsh are the ones he loves.

Os hwylia fe'n haelaidd gylch Dehau'n ddiduedd,
Neu fyned i'r Gogledd, hyd Wynedd ddiwarth;
Daw'r bonedd godidog, a'r beirdd yn galonnog
I roesaw da *Hebog* Deheubarth.

        Should he sail more freely around south [Wales],
        Or go to the North, to faultless Gwynedd,
        The fine gentry and the cheerful bards will gather
        To greet warmly Hebog of Deheubarth.

Oddiamgylch eu byrddau, gwresogion eu seigiau,
Fe gaiff historiau'n hen deidiau, wyr da,
A chywydd ac englyn, ac awdlau Taliesin,
A chwrw haidd melyn ei wala.

Around their tables, laden with hot dishes,
He will hear tell of our ancestor, splendid folk,
And a cywydd and englyn, and the odes of Taliesin,
With golden barley beer aplenty.

Er llesiant croesawus cymdeithas gariadus,
Dychweled ein Ustus yn drefnus i'w dre'
Rhag digwydd i fradwr, trwy'r cwmwd wneud cynnwr',
Tra byddo'n Rheolwr dan hwyliau.

For the good of a devoted community
May our Justice return speedily to his home,
Lest a traitor should cause commotion in the commot
While our Governor is away under sail.

Yr awr y dychwelo, rho'ir clych i gydseinio,
Trwy Gemais yn gryno, pan dirio o'r dŵr,
A'r bobloedd yn dyfod, hyd for i'w gyfarfod,
Ond iddynt gael gwybod o Geibwr.

The moment he retirns, bells will be ringing
Throughout the land of Cemais, when he sets foot on land;
The people will flock to the seashore to greet him,
Once they receive the good news from Ceibwr.[31]

Ioan Siencyn

John Grono

(1767-1847)

John Grono, described as 'a burly blue-eyed Pembrokeshire Welsh-man',was born in Newport in 1767, a member of the local family of Gronow whose name was misspelt from the time he first appears, on 17 January 1794, as an able-bodied seaman having been wounded while serving on HMS *Venus* and being awarded a pension of £5 per annum from the Naval Chest at Chatham. He had been married at the Thames-side Rotherhithe Parish Church on 20 July 1790 to Elizabeth Bristow by whom he had seven daughters and five sons. In 1798 he sailed to Australia as a boatswain's mate on the armed supply ship HMS *Buffalo* (the figurehead of which, nonetheless, was a kangaroo), taking with him his wife and two daughters and leaving their son, John, with his maternal grandmother at Bristol. The ship arrived at Port Jackson on 3 May 1799 where Grono found employment as first officer of the *Francis*, a 44 ton government sloop rigged as a schooner, that was said to have been the first ship built in Australia, its component parts having been brought from England.

By 1802 he had settled on a small farm, which he called Grono Park, situated near Windsor on the fertile flood plain of the river Hawkesbury, and in the following year he purchased land that pro-vided him with a frontage on to the river, which became known as Grono's Point. He received further grants of land, one of which he requested so that he and his sons 'could have recourse for Blue Gum for ship building.'[32]

New South Wales was still largely a penal settlement and ship building was not allowed lest it should provide convicts with the means of escape but, in view of the absence of roads and the short-age of beasts of burden, it became necessary to provide craft to transport commodities along the river between the isolated settle-ments on the Hawkesbury and Sydney. In 1802 Andrew Thompson, an ex-convict who had been pardoned and appointed chief constable, was able to enter the shipping trade by acquiring the 16 ton sloop *Hope*. Two years later, John Grono purchased a sloop of 18 tons, the *Speedwell*, which ran aground soon afterwards and he sold her to Thompson who sent her sealing. In 1805 Grono set off on a sealing expedition in the *Ferret*, accompanied by his compatriot Evan Evans, and completed a successful voyage. He then began to build his own ships, beginning with a 100 ton schooner that was launched on 4 April 1807 and named *Governor Bligh* after William Bligh, the former Captain Bligh of the *Bounty*, who had been appointed Governor of New South Wales and had farming interests along the Hawkesbury. In August the following year, with Grono as master, the vessel went sealing off the southern coasts of New Zealand and returned a year later bringing upwards of ten thousand seal skins, which were sold for 4s.6d. (42p) each. Between then and 1819 he brought back such quantities of seal skins and elephant seal oil that he was referred to as 'the most famous sealer in the early colonial history of Australia.'

His account of this voyage provided the first evidence of the existence of an island, Stewart Island, off the southernmost point of New Zealand, which Captain Cook had omitted to mark on his charts. Grono described the stretch of water separating the island from the mainland as 'a very dangerous navigation from the numerous rocks, shoals, and little islands with which it is crowded'[31] and he named it Foveaux Strait after Colonel Foveaux who had arrived in July 1808 as Lieutenant-Governor only to find that Bligh had been deposed by the people and kept under arrest on HMS *Porpoise*.[33]

On 15 December 1813, after sealing for sixteen months, Grono returned to Sydney with 14,000 seal skins and five tons of elephant oil, along with ten men, members of a sealing gang that had been marooned on Secretary Island since February 1810. Their brig, the *Active*, had gone to Port Jackson for provisions but had never returned and the men had subsisted on seal meat, infrequently caught fish and sea birds, and the root of a rare fern. They had been rescued by Grono and three of their number later married three of his daughters.

Grono relinquished command of the *Governor Bligh* in 1819 and the ship was sold, but when it arrived in Sydney fourteen years later, it was still described as one of 'the twelve vessels built by our old Colonial Neptune'. He spent the next two years building a brig of

130 tons, named *Elizabeth* after his wife, that was launched in 1821 and he took her on her maiden voyage to New Zealand where, in a cave on Cape Providence, a stone was later found upon which he had carved the words 'John Grono brig Elizabeth'. The cave is now known as Grono Cave and the stone is in the Southland Museum.

Grono's name also survives in Mount Grono, on Secretary Island, in Gronow's (*sic*) Sound, and in Grono Bay, where he had his sealing station. He named the nearby Thompson and Nancy Sounds after his friend Andrew Thompson and his wife, and also Bligh Sound and Mutimy Peak and Bounty Haven, despite the local opinion of Bligh.[34] It is claimed that he gave its name to the magnificent fiord-like Milford Sound,[35] the direction to which he gave to the cartographer Jules de Blosseville in 1824. He called it Milford Haven but the name was changed to Milford Sound by Admiral John Lort Stokes of Scotchwells, Haverfordwest, when he surveyd the New Zealand coast in 1851.

In 1827 Grono retired from the sea and he is shown in the 1828 census as a successful land owner possessing over three thousand acres and running 309 head of cattle and 205 sheep, but he then suffered under a depression that hit New South Wales. In 1842 he offered his estate for sale but it was not finally sold until 1853 by which time his real estate was heavily mortgaged. He was able to retain Grono Park, however, and lived there for the rest of his life.

He was one of the founders of Ebenezer Chapel built on the Hawkesbury River in 1809, the first Presbyterian church erected in Australia. When a death took place, a funeral procession of boats conveyed the departed on the river to the cemetery beside the church, the leading boat, with muffled oars, towing the boat carrying the coffin, and the mourners followed in mourning craft to a small sandy beach close to the chapel that provided a convenient landing place. John Grono died on 4 May 1847 and was buried at Ebenezer where a fine table tomb, raised to his memory and that of his wife, Elizabeth, stands prominently beside the chapel door.

It would be engaging to consider that the chapel had been named after Ebenezer Congregational Chapel at Newport, with which the Gronow family was associated until the middle of the last century when Ebenezer Richard Gronow was the precentor, but there is no evidence that this was so.

Y Shah

The *Shah* was a horse-drawn coach owned by Richard Jackson, land-lord of the Prince of Wales Hotel, now Llysmeddyg, and afterwards of the Queen's Hotel, Parrog. It was later bought by **William Davies** (1837-1907), master mariner and proprietor of the of the Commercial (Castle) Hotel from where it ran daily to Crymych, the nearest railway station at that time. It was regularly used by sailors leaving home, or returning from sea. **John Ernest Morris** (p. 79) would preface one of his stories by asking: 'Did I tell you about the time we got drunk before we got to Australia?' and on receiving the expected negative reply he would proceed: 'Matter of fact, we got drunk before we got to Crymych!' Mrs Anne Hughes-Rees, who died in 1990 aged 102 years, informed the author that she recalled being taken as a small child on the coach taking her father, **James Davies** (1859-1954), master mariner, back to sea in 1892.

The poem was written by the Rev. John Jones (Iohannes Towy), who had been removed from his church and had become an itinerant cleric, so that he travelled much in the coach. He lodged with Elizabeth, widow of **John Davies** (1826-74) at Woodfield, Churh Street. The author last heard the poem sung in its entirety by **James Thomas Isaac** in January 1952.

Y SHAH

Mae'r corn yn bloeddio, Be' sy'n bod?
Y Shah, y cerbyd mawr, sy'n dod
Ar bedair o olwynion cryf
Yn llusgo llwythi trwm yn hyf.

The post-horn blares. What can it be?
The great coach, Shah, is coming by;
On four hard-wearing wheels
Hauling huge loads without effort.

Mor hardd, mor nerthol yw *Y Shah*;
Mor gyflym ac mor ddewr yr â,
O Drefdraeth fwyn i Grymych lân
Y rhed i gwrdd â'r cerbyd tân.

So handsome, so well-built, is the Shah,
So swiftly and so bold it travels
From gentle Newport to fair Crymych
Where it meets the 'fire-driven horse'.

A chluda deithwyr ar eu taith
I ddŵr y môr o bellter maith;
Saeson, Cymry, iach a chlaf
Ddont gyda'r *Shah* ar ddydd o haf.

It carries travellers on their journey
To the seaside from distant places.
Both English and Welsh, healthy and ailing
Come on the Shah on a summer's day.

A golygfeydd rhyfeddol iawn
Ar hyd y ffordd i gyd a gawn –
Bryniau, coedydd, dolau gwyrdd
A rhyfeddodau anian fyrdd.

The most beautiful scenery
Is enjoyed along the way:
Hills, forests, green meadows
Along with the wonders of nature

Trwy Eglwyswrw y mae'n hardd,
Ac yn Felindre mae fel gardd.
Swynol a hyfryd yw mewn gair
O Grymych fryniog i Lwyngwair.

By Eglwyswrw it is beautiful,
And Felindre is like a garden;
Alluring and agreeable, in a word,
From hilly Crymych to Llwyngwair.

Ar fin y ffordd y Nyfer lân,
Yn treiglo tua'r môr ymla'n,
Glwys afon loew enwog yw:
Ar fin yr hon fu Tegid byw.

> *Beside the road, the splendid Nevern*
> *Flows onward towards the sea,*
> *Fair, crystal-clear river, it is famous:*
> *Upon its banks the poet Tegid lived.*

Bloedded yr utgorn megis cawr,
A'r môr yn dod i'r golwg nawr;
I'r preseb â y ddau farch da
A boed llonyddwch heno i'r *Shah*.

> *Let the horn blow a gigantic blast*
> *As the sea now comes into sight.*
> *To the stable the stallions will go,*
> *And the Shah is put to rest for the night.*

Y morwr wedi teithio'r byd
Ddaw gyda'r *Shah* mewn llawen fryd,
I weld y tŷ a'i wraig a'r plant
Fu ar ei gof amserau gant.

> *The mariner, having travelling the world,*
> *Arrives with the Shah, full of joy*
> *At seeing his home, his wife, his children,*
> *That were in his mind all the time.*

Ac O'r llawenydd sydd gerllaw –
Cusanu, gwenu ac ysgwyd llaw;
Y morwr wedi dod yn iach
I ail gofleidio ei rai bach.

> *And Oh! The happiness now at hand:*
> *Kisses, smiles, and handshakes,*
> *The sailor home from the sea*
> *Able to caress his little ones.*

Meddyliodd am eu gwedd a'u hynt
Pan ar y môr mewn stormydd gwynt,
Myfyriai ef amdanynt hwy
Pan ruthrai'r storom eto'n fwy.

> *Their daily lives possessed his thoughts*
> *Whilst on the sea in stormy weather;*
> *They were in his meditations*
> *As the storm grew ever louder.*

Pan gwyd y môr ei donnau mawr
Yn ddŵr fynyddau hyll eu gwawr,
Fe gofia'r morwr y pryd hyn
Am wraig ei fron a'i blentyn gwyn.

> *When the sea rises into huge waves,*
> *Like mountains of water hideous to behold,*
> *The sailor at this time, remembers*
> *The wife of his bosom and his blessed child.*

Pan 'n ôl i'r môr y morwr â,
Rhaid cychwyn eto gyda'r *Shah*,
Rhaid codi'n fore gyda'r wawr
I wynebu Lerpwl fawr.

> *When the time comes to return to the sea,*
> *The sailor must again seek the Shah,*
> *Rise in the morning, at the crack of dawn*
> *And turn his face towards Liverpool.*

Ti forwr hwylus fron,
Duw fo'th Dad ar frig y don;
Bydd dithau'n ufudd iddo Ef
Tra'n morio ar dy daith i'r Nef.

> *Thou, sailor, happy at heart,*
> *May God be thy Father on the crest of the wave:*
> *Be obedient unto Him*
> *While sailing on the journey to Heaven.*

Iohannes Towy

Parrog House

Parrog House is conspicuous as the only three-storey Georgian house on the Parrog. It is listed by *Cadw*: Welsh Historic Monuments as 'an "early 19th century" large house, now subdivided' which may support the date 1827 found on a beam and on walls beneath plaster during renovations in 1990. By the 1880s the house had been split in half, the eastern part retaining the name Parrog House and the western half was called Sunnymead. The division had been made by removing the Georgian staircase and building a partition wall, with separate stairs on each side of it. The wall fell short of reaching the tall arched window at the back of the house leaving a narrow gap so that the occupants of one house could hear a person on the stairs of the other.

In about 1890 the house was purchased by Dr Peter Maurice Griffiths Williams, a retired London surgeon born in Little New-castle and descended from Williams of Trearched in the parish of Llanrhian. He married Mary Grace, daughter of John James, master mariner, of Parrog, at St Mary's Church on 18 November 1861 and had two sons, George Hugh Meredith, and John Daniel Evans, and three daughters: Grace Mary, Elgina Alberta and Margaret Gwendoline. Peter Williams died in 1910 and he and his wife, who had predeceased him in 1898, are commemorated in stained glass windows in the chancel of St Mary's. The eldest daughter, Grace Mary, a spinster, lived at Parrog House with her sister Gwendoline until, in her latter days, she moved to Castle Hill, Fishguard, the home of her married sister, Elgina.

Gwendoline married Ivor Llewellyn Williams, master mariner, who had been born in Cardigan in 1874 and they lived at Sunnymead. Ivor was invariably dressed in a dark grey jersey, shirt and tie and dark grey knickerbockers, and golf shoes with trefoil metal studs. He hardly ever wore a hat or a cap, and his hair was short and dark grey. Gwennie as he called her, was a buxom lady who was hardly ever seen other than sitting in their open pale grey Darracq car in which they drove out on sunny days. On Thursdays they took tea with the rector at The Court, now Gelli Olau.

Gwennie was against the drink and Ivor had to resort to various ploys in order to have the odd noggin. When the car reached Fishguard Square, it broke down and Ivor would say to Gwennie: 'Trouble with the engine, my dear. I shall have to borrow a spanner from the Misses Rees.' The Misses Rees kept the Commercial (now the Abergwaun) Hotel. He would return with the spanner, tinker under the bonnet and return the spanner, by which time the Misses Rees would have a large pink gin ready for him to knock back.

When he took her to dinner at the Ivy Bush in Carmarthen on one occasion, half way through the meal he excused himself saying: 'Pardon me, my dear, a call of nature you know.' In those days the bar was just outside the dining room and Stanley Thomas, the landlord, would have been briefed to have a large gin ready for Ivor to consume, which he did marking time on the flagstone floor in his hob nailed shoes so that Gwennie would think that he was on his way to the Gents.

He was a regular customer at the Queen's on the Parrog. During the 1914 war, presumably when he was on leave, he made his regular call there one morning but Mrs Edwards, the landlady, had to inform him that she was out of gin but that a small cask found on the beach contained a spirit which, she was told, tasted just like gin. 'I'll try a glass, Mrs Edwards,' said Ivor and agreed with her that it did taste like gin, and called for another. As usual, he produced a small bottle that he carried in his trousers pocket so as to drink secretly at home. Mrs Edwards filled the bottle which he put in his pocket. He then collapsed and had to be carried home where he was confined to his bed for some days. During that time, Gwennie found the bottle in his pocket and, assuming that it was a cleaning fluid, she used it to clean some marks on his trousers and hung them on the clothes line to dry. When she took them off the line she noticed that the patches that she had cleaned were now holes.

When Gwennie died in 1935, Ivor had a stone column placed on her grave bearing a copper-faced sundial and inscribed: 'Sunny Hours. Latitude 52° 54' North Longitude 4° 48' West' and on the stone the words: 'Margaret Gwendoline, beloved wife of Ivor Ll. Williams, Sunnymead, Newport. Died 16. 3. 35. Abide with Me.'

After Gwennie had died, Ivor married Mrs Lindstrum, the widow of a Russian Finn who had been brought to this country during the 1914 war to cut down the trees in Llwyngwair Woods. She kept a small shop by the limekiln-keeper's house on the Parrog and, being Jewish, she kept it open on Sundays. She gave up the shop and he sold Sunnymead and they went to live at Solva, where he died.

Elgina Alberta married Walter John Vaughan, solicitor, Castle Hill, Fishguard, down the road from his rival, Mr Vincent Johns, solicitor and Clerk of the Peace. Vaughan would be seen moving excitedly along the street, a Jimminy Cricket-like figure, aptly known as Vaughan Bach. According to a story told at Fishguard, he once appointed a junior clerk who started work on a day when he had a bad hangover. The boy brought him the mail and asked: 'What shall I do now, sir?' Vaughan impatiently said: 'Oh, go and stack the books.' The boy returned more than once with a similar request and each time his master grew more irritable until, finally, when the boy asked: 'What shall I do now, sir?' Vaughan burst out and screamed: 'Oh go and stick your backside out of the window!' The boy went back upstairs to his office that was facing the street and did as he had been told. After a time, he returned to his master who, by now, was somewhat more composed, and said: 'I have done that, sir. What shall I do now?' 'Done what, boy, done what?' Vaughan enquired: 'I put my backside out of the window as you said, sir.' 'Good God – you stupid boy – did anyone see you?' 'Only Mr Vincent Johns, sir. He looked up and said, "Good morning, Mr Vaughan."'

The house was occupied in the 1920s by David Richards, former coachman at Llwyngwair, who had been severely wounded in the 1914-18 war and had lost an eye. His eldest daughter, Doreen, became a well known professional singer under the name Grace Nevern.

Ships trading at Newport
pre-1876

Owner or Main owner

Ann and Betsey, smack, 22 tons, 1837 .... Elizabeth Berriman
Ann and Mary, sloop, 22 tons, 1762 .... Thomas Davies
Ardent, snow, 120 tons, 1800.
Cambria, sloop, 25 tons, built Abercastle 1793.
    Lost 1835 .... Thomas Mathias
Castle Malgwyn, schooner, 100 tons,
    built Cardigan 1800 .... Daniel Evans
Ceturah, 'the first brig builkt at this port' .... David Gilbert
Charlotte, schooner, 81 tons, 1824 .... David Harries
Charming Peggy, sloop, 63 tons, 1789 .... John Bowsher & others
Commerce, sloop, 35 tons, built Carmarthen 1800 ... John Phillips
David, schooner, 26 tons, 1830.
Eliza, sloop, 16 tons, built Berkeley, Glos. 1822.
Eliza, schooner, 160 tons, built Milford .... William Davies
Excel, brig, 230 tons, built Milford 1854.
Exley, sloop, 29 tons, built Hull 1840.
    Lost 1871 off Strumble Head .... Elizabeth Berriman
Fly, smack, 23 tons, built Aberaeron 1860 .... Richard Jackson
Frances, sloop, 33 tons, built Aberporth 1808,
    transferred to Newport 1837 .... D. Evans
Friendship, brig, 83 tons, 1817.
Greyhound, schooner, *c.*30 tons,
    built Aberystwyth *c.*1770 .... Thomas Lloyd, Cwmgloyn
Hawk, schooner, 50 tons, built at
    Newport *c.*1771 .... Thomas Lloyd, Cwmgloyn
Hope, sloop, 42 tons, 1812 .... Henry Vaughan
Hope, brig, 155 tons, built Swansea 1813 .... John Harries
Hopewell, sloop, 18 tons, built New Quay 1810.
    Lost 1852 at Fishguard .... David Jones

Jane & Catherine, sloop, 29 tons, built Conway
   1837 .... Thomas Rees
Jane & Margaret, sloop, 24 tons, built Llansanffraid,
   Denb. 1859 .... William Evans
John, sloop, 16 tons, built Milford 1838 .... Ann Jones
John, schooner, 70 tons, built Bridgwater 1777 .... D. Gilbert
John, sloop, 28 tons, built Milford 1828. Lost 1845 ... John Davies
Margaret, snow, 128 tons, built Milford 1830.
   Lost 1830 Baltic-London .... J. & Thos. Davies
Maria, schooner, 64 tons, built New Quay 1849,
   sold to Newport 1864.
Mary & Eliza, sloop, 129 tons, built Carmarthen 1824.
   Lost 1832 .... John Davies
Neptune, smack, 32 tons, built Bristol 1827.
   Run down by steamer, Isle of Man 1849 .... Llew Evans
Oak, flat, 33 tons, built Queensferry 1840 .... J. Davies
Pheasant, sloop, 25 tons, built New Quay 1837.
   Wrecked Hellsmouth 1864 .... E. Jones
Prince Regent, sloop, 31 tons, built Solva 1813 ..... Daniel Evans
Richard & Mary, smack, 18 tons,
   built Pembroke Dock 1848 .... Elizabeth Berriman
Royal Recovery, brig, 82 tons, built Kidwelly.
   Lost 1832 .... R. Morris
Sarah, schooner, 124 tons, built Cardigan 1842 .... David Thomas
Speculator, schooner, 76 tons, built Aberystwyth
   1804 .... David Jones
Tit Bit, brigantine, 133 tons, built Bridport 1849 .. Thomas Jenkins
Twenty Two, sloop, 31 tons, built Cardiff 1822 ...... William Rees

Ships trading at Newport 1876-1900

o/ indicates owner or part owner, *m/* master, *o&m/* owner and master

Adeona, schooner, 24 tons, built New Quay 1825, *o/* Thos. Bidder, *m/* Joseph Williams.

Aeron, smack, 17 tons, built Aberporth, *o&m/* Jacob Beer.

Albatross, smack, 28 tons, built Aberaeron 1864, *o/* H. Howell, *m/* John James.

Albion, dandy, 46 tons, built Aberaeron 1827, *o&m/* James Deeble.

Alice, steamer, 96 tons, *o&m/* William Myers.

Andes, smack, 35 tons, *o&m/* John Williams.

Ann, sloop, 23 tons, built Cardigan 1825, *o/* David Rowlands, *m/* Joseph Williams.

Ann Maria, smack, 26 tons, *o/* John Thomas, *m/* John Minchinton.

Ann & Betsey, smack, 15 tons, built Newport 1837, *o/* Elizabeth Berriman, *m/* Samuel Jenkins.

Annie, schooner, 65 tons, *o/* T. Philemor, *m/* H. Nicholas.

Aquila, ketch, 74 tons, *o/* J. Bentley, *m/* W. Pollock.

Aurora, smack, 30 tons, *o&m/* J Thomas.

Band of Hope, yacht, 12 tons, *o/* W. Hunter, *m/* E. Wright, cruising in ballast.

Berthon, canvas collapsing yawl, *o/* Berthon & Co., Romsey, *m/* A. W. Cooke, on experimental voyage from Southampton to Liverpool suffering stress of weather.

Beryl, smack, 36 tons, built Aberarth 1841.

Britannia, smack, 30 tons, built Aberporth 1793, *o/* Anne Rowe, *m/* James Evans.

Charming Nancy, smack, 21 tons, built Milford 1827, *o/* Thomas Platt, *m/* J. Evans, lost off Dee Light 1909.

Christianna, smack, 25 tons, built Pembroke Dock 1837, lost off Penbryn 1896, *o/* Wm. Wood, *m/* John Morris.

Cristal, sloop, *o&m/* Jacob Beer.

Clara, smack, 40 tons, *o&m/* D. Davies.

Commerce, sloop, 35 tons, built Carmarthen 1800, *o/* John Phillips, *m/* Jenkin Thomas 1877.

Cymro, smack, 28 tons, built Milford 1888, lost 1902, *o/* Wm. Francis, *m/* J. Williams.

Daring, schooner, 82 tons, *m/* J. Stribling from Lydney.

David, smack, 26 tons, built Newport, *o/* Thos. Edwards, *m/* Wm. Edwards.

Dovey Packet, smack, 28 tons, *o/* T. Doughton, *m/* John Thomas.

Eagle, smack, 23 tons, built New Quay 1838, lost off Strumble Head 1884, *o&m/* Jenkin Davies.

Edith Williams, smack, 24 tons, *o/* W. Williams, *m/* G. Richards.

Eleanor, smack, 19 tons, built Cwmtudu 1826, *o&m/* John Jones.

Eliza Anne, smack, 31 tons, built New Quay 1877, sunk by submarine 40 miles SE of Lizard, November 1918, *o&m/* David Evans.

Elizabeth, sloop, 35 tons, built Cardigan 1844, foundered Eddystone 1891, *o&m/* Evan Williams.

Elizabeth Davies, smack, 28 tons, built Cardigan 1868, lost off Irish coast 1878, *o&m/* W. Jones.

Ellen, smack, 26 tons, built Aberaeron 1852, *o&m/* David Evans.

Ellendole, smack, 19 tons, from Milford with Patent Manure, *o&m/* J. Williams.

Emily, smack, 18 tons, *o/* Pierce Llewelyn, *m/* James Williams.

Fanny, smack, 16 tons, *o&m/* George Beddoe.

Farmer's Lass, smack, 27 tons, built Aberaeron 1859, wrecked off Bude 1902, *o&m/* J. Owen.

Favourite, smack, 34 tons, *o/* T. Hurlow, *m/* John Davies.

Flying Dutchman, dandy, 57 tons, *m/* Wm. Williams, from Newport, Gwent, with coal.

Frances, sloop, 33 tons, built Aberporth 1808, transferred to Newport 1837, *o/* David Evans.

Friends, smack, 24 tons, *o/* H. Hole, *m/* L. Allen, from Lydney with coal.

Gauntlet, schooner, 109 tons, *o/* Jas Fisher, *m/* J. Selby, Barrow-Rotterdam, called for shelter.

Gausillipo, smack, 34 tons, *o&m/* J. Jones.

Gecheries Francais, dandy, 42 tons, *o/* J. Rowlands, *m/* S. Phillips, culm from Nolton.

George Evans, ketch, 32 tons, built New Quay 1862, broken up 1921, *o&m/* Thomas Thomas.

Gloucester Packet, smack, 22 tons, built Carmarthen 1836, *o/* R. Jackson, *m/* Stephen Lewis.

Glyndwr, schooner, 26 tons, *o&m/* J. Williams, from Lydney with coal.

Good Hope, sloop, 25 tons, built Aberystwyth 1825, *o/* J. Beer, *m/* D. Davies.

Heatherbell, dandy, 57 tons, built Cardigan 1873, *o/* Thos. Davies, *m/* David Rees.

James, ketch, 44 tons, *o&m/* J. Boon.

Jane, smack, 28 tons, built Aberporth 1787, *o&m/* Thos. Morgan.

Jane & Margaret, sloop, 24 tons, built Llansantffraid, Denbigh 1859, *o/* Wm Evans, *m/* John Thomas.

Jedulous, schooner, 67 tons, *o&m/* Humphrey Roberts.

Jenny, sloop, 23 tons, built New Quay, lost Newport 1840.

John & Elizabeth, smack, 21 tons, built Milford 1849, *o/* L. Phillips, *m/* Ellis Griffiths.

John George, smack, 36 tons, *o&m/* David Lewis.

Kate, smack, 25 tons, *o/* John Llewellin Davies, *m/* David Roberts.

Kitten, smack, 41 tons, *m/* A. C. Flanders, from Glasgow, windbound & machinery out of order.

Lady Brassey, steam launch, 6 tons, *o/* W. Hoher, *m/* J. Beer, from Haverfordwest.

Lady Mary, smack, 29 tons, *o/* J. Thomas, *m/* W. Davies.

Lerry, smack, 38 tons, *o&m/* Morris Davies.

Lizzie Ann, smack, 24 tons, *o&m/* Wm. Williams.

Little Malta, smack, *o&m/* J. Tedwell.

Lord Exmouth, smack, 19 tons, *o&m/* Dd. Thomas, from Haverfordwest.

Margaret Alice, smack, 26 tons, *o&m/* J. Russan.

Margaret & Ann, smack, 28 tons, built Aberystwyth 1843, *o/* Owen Jones, *m/* Evan Parry, broken up 1918.

Margaret Ellen, smack, 27 tons, built Cardigan 1872, *o&m/* Thomas Davies, sailed until 1922.

Margaret Lewis, smack, 28 tons, built Cardigan 1869, *o/* J. Hughes, *m/* D. Thomas, lost with all hands off South Stack 1904.

Margaretta, smack, 25 tons, *o&m/* Evan Rees.

Martha Jane, smack, 17 tons, *o&m/* John Jones.

Martha Jane, smack, 28 tons, built Aberaeron 1861, wrecked off Llannon 1903, *o/* J. Tudor, *m/* J. Williams.

Mary, smack, 21 tons, *o&m/* John Morgan.

Mary Ann, smack, 22 tons, built Newport 1816, *o/* J. Evans, *m/* J. Morris.

Mary Jane, smack, 28 tons, built Cardigan 1868, *o&m/* D. Jenkins.

Merganser, steam yacht, 25 tons, *o/* T. Pender, MP *m/* J. Pursdon, Loch Foyle-London, came for shelter for the night, 14 Sept. 1890.

Miss Sarah, smack, 15 tons, *o/* Wm. Thomas, *m/* Daniel Evans, lost off St Ann's Head 1877.

Mountain Maid, smack, 26 tons, *o&m/* Thos. Lamb.

Muriel, 5 ton yacht belonging to General Sturt, Newport Castle, *m/* W. Taylor, taking ballast.

Myrtle, smack, 25 tons, *o&m/* Wm. Edwards.

Newland, dandy, 28 tons, *o&m/* Jacob Beer.

New Providence, schooner, 32 tons, *o&m/* Jacob Beer.

Ocean, smack, 33 tons, built Aberaeron 1827, *o&m/* Thomas Davies, lost Cardigan Bar 1895.

Pamela Pennant, smack, 29 tons, *o&m/* Levi Francis.

Penelope, smack, 27 tons, o&m /Levi Harries.

Phoenix, smack, 27 tons, *o&m/* Levi Harries.

Phoenix, smack, 23 tons, *o/* Mary Thomas, *m/* Stephen Lewis.

Price Jones, flat, 23 tons, built in Flint 1859, *o/* Thomas Roach, *m/* Wm. Williams.

Pride of Wales, smack, 31 tons, *o/* H. G. Jones, *m/* D. Morgan.

Princess Louisa, ketch, 19 tons, *o/* G. Lewis, *m/* S. Phillips.

Punch, smack, 23 tons, *o&m/* John Thomas.

Rechabite, smack, 18 tons, *o&m/* Jacob Beer.

Regina, dandy, 41 tons, *o&m/* J. Russan.

Resolution, smack, 39 tons, built Aberaeron 1865, *o&m/* David Thomas.

Richard & Mary, smack, 18 tons, built Pembroke Dock 1848.

Rose, sloop, 37 tons, built Cardigan 1798, *o&m/* Henry Johns.

Sarah, smack, 27 tons, built Cowes 1797, *o/* John Williams, *m/* George Lile.

Sarah, schooner, 124 tons, built Cardigan 1842, *o/* David Thomas.

Sarah Ann, smack, 23 tons, *o&m/* Wm. George.

Sarah of Scarbro, dandy, 25 tons, *o&m/* Wm. Davies.

Seaflower, 62 ton steamer, built Glasgow 1875, Cardigan-Bristol, called to discharge 5 tons, guano 1888.

Sea Prince, tug boat, Liverpool-Cardiff, called for coal 1888.

Secret, dandy, 63 tons, *o/* J. Trine, *m/* W. Thomas, from Gloucester with manure.

Seven Brothers, smack, 47 tons, *o/* J. Loyd, *m/* W. Hensen from Newport, Gwent, with coal.

Speculator, schooner, 76 tons, built Aberystwyth 1804, *o/* David Jones.

Speedwell, smack, 22 tons, built Llangrannog 1822, *o/* T. Canton, *m/* J. Mathias.

Spread Eagle, smack, 26 tons, built Llanina 1814, *o&m/* David Jenkins.

Thomas, smack, 26 tons, built Padstow 1859, lost off St Govans 1892, *o&m/* D. Davies.

Thiomas of Liverpool, schooner, 63 tons, *o/* S. C. Cooper, *m/* John Jones.

Tivyside, steamer, 62 tons, built Govan 1869, *o/* T. Davies, *m/* J. Owens, wrecked near Port Eynon 1900.

Triumph, dandy, 46 tons, *o/* J. Turnidge, *m/* W. Bond, from London with manure.

Try, smack, 27 tons, *o/* Wm. Davies, *m/* David Davies.

Unity, smack, 34 tons, built New Quay, *o&m/* John Davies.

Vandora, steamer, 73 tons, *o/* S. Steele, *m/* T. Davies.

Wave Queen, dandy, 33 tons, *o/* P. Vittle, *m/* H. Vittle.

William & Maria, smack, 25 tons, *o&m/* Wm. Lamb.

Willie Percy, smack, 14 tons, *o/* R. Chrimes, *m/* T. Lewis.

Notes

1. *The Ancient Borough of Newport in Pembrokeshire*, Dillwyn Miles, Haverfordwest 1995, 2nd ed. 1998, 3.

2. Parrog, from the Old English *pearroc* meaning 'a small enclosure, paddock which has developed a new specific sense of "flat land along the shore" (?used for unloading boats) in south Wales.' It was the name for a landing place for ships in Swansea, and for a fishing enclosure in Essex, *The Place-names of Pembrokeshire*, B. G. Charles, National Library of Wales 1992, p. 165. The author heard a boatman refer to the pebble beach on Ramsey Island as 'the parrog'. The shingle bank at Newgale and a beach of pebble stones at Saundersfoot are known as the Paddock.

3. *Calendar of the Public Records relating to Pembrokeshire*, ed. Henry Owen, Vol. III, London 1918, 245-6.

4. 'The Economy 1536-1642' by Brian Howells in *Pembrokeshire County History*, Vol. III, Haverfordwest 1987, 91. It is interesting to note that John Roberts, born within the boundaries of Cemais, at Little Newcastle in 1682, went to sea as a boy and became the famous pirate, Bartholomew Roberts, whom Daniel Defoe regarded as the most successful of all pirates, having captured more than four hundred ships.

5. *The Welsh Port Books (1550-1603)*, ed. E. A. Lewis, London, 1927, 311-5.

6. *ibid.* 83, 84 and 99.

7. *The Description of Pembrokeshire: George Owen of Henllys*, ed. Dillwyn Miles, Gomer Press, 1994, 46.

8. *ibid.* 149.

9. *ibid.* 119.

10. *Gerald of Wales: The Journey through Wales*, ed. Lewis Thorpe, Penguin, 1988, 173.

11. *The Ancient Borough of Newport*, 64-6.

12. *The Description of Pembrokeshire*, 60, 123-4, 139-40, 269

13. *Report on the Harbours and Customs Administration of Wales under Edward VI* (1547-53), Thomas Phaer.

14. *Plans of Harbours Bars, Bays and Roads in St George's Channel*, Lewis Morris 1748, plate 19, (Newport Bay & Harbour) and plate 26 which has a drawing of 'a Porcupine to clear old Bars', an implement that looks like a horse-drawn roller covered with spikes, being towed by a boat.

15. *The Description of Pembrokeshire*, 71.

16. The *Newport Boarding Book 1876-1900* was in the possession of Vincent Morris, Glan-y-don, Parrog, who published extracts from it in the *County Echo* in 1958. After his death it came into the possession of his nephew, John P. Morris, who has deposited the manuscript at the Pembrokeshire Record Office.

17. 'The Davieses of Newport and Cardigan: The Founding of a Dynasty' by Donald Davies in *Those Were the Days: A History of Cardigan and the Locality*, 1992, vol. 2, 1-22.
    Strangers from a Strange Land, Peter Thomas, Gomer Press 1986, 6 *passim*.

18. 'Pembrokeshire Trading' by Barbara J. George, in *Field Studies*, vol. 2, no. 1, 1964, 33-4.

19. *Maritime Heritage*, J. Geraint Jenkins, Gomer Press, 1982, 83-96.

20. *Deadly Perils*, Peter S. Davies, Merrivale Press, 2nd ed. 1999, 42-5.

21. 'Departed Glory' by Lloyd Richards, in *Newport Regatta Almanack and Year Book*, 1958, 15.

22. 'The Voyage of the Brig *Albion* with Emigrants from Caernarvonshire to North America' by Dr Llywelyn Wyn-Griffith, in *Maritime Wales* 5, 1980, 31-42. A pamphlet giving 'An account of the Voyage of the brig *Albion* of Cardigan (Llywelyn Davies, Master) with emigrants, etc., from Caernarvon to North America' published by Peter Evans, Caernarfon, in 1820, was found by Dr Griffith in Will Griffiths' book shop in Cecil Court, London in 1959 and was drawn upon by him while writing his novel *The Way Lies West*. The ruined castle had the two gatehouse towers as one of them had not yet been taken down in order to build the present residence.

23. *A Minglèd Yarn, Recollections*, Dillwyn Miles, Dinefwr Press, 2000, 222.

24. *Dewsland and Kemes Guardian*, 2 June 1877.

25. 'Dunkirk – The Fishguard Connection' by Robin Evans, in the *The County Echo*, 21 January 1994.

26. *A Mingled Yarn*, 205.

27. *ibid.* 206.

28. 'The Last of the Traditional Storytellers 1851-1930' by Dillwyn Miles, in *The Journal of the Pembrokeshire Historical Society*, No. 13, 2004, 60, 63.

29. *Blodau Dyfed*, Carmarthen 1824, 214-6. The poem is written in *mesur y tri-thrawiad* (the three beat measure), in which the words in the middle of the first line, at the end of the first line and in the middle of the second line, rhyme with each other. The words at the ends of the third and fourth lines also rhyme. The poet uses touches of *cynghanedd*, which was defined some four hundred years ago as 'the correspondence of consonants and interchange of vowels', and no one has been able to provide a clearer definition. *The Royal National Eisteddfod of Wales*, Dillwyn Miles, Swansea, 1978, 149-61.

30. *A Book of Wales*, ed. D. M. & E. M. Lloyd, Collins, 114.

31. Ceibwr is the nearest bay north of Newport where a boat could land and from which a runner could take a message to Newport.

32. *Two Lawless Sailors*, Grono-Books Association, Richmond, NSW, 1984, 14-33.

33. *Murihiku*, Robert McNab, Invercargill, NSW, 1907, 102.

34. *Macquarie Country*, D. G. Bowd, Griffin Press, Netley, 1973, 26.

35. *Fïordland Explored*, John Hall-Jones, Invercargill, NSW, 1979.